the story of the U.S.A.

by Franklin Escher, Jr.

Book 4
Modern America

EDUCATORS PUBLISHING SERVICE
Cambridge and Toronto

Printed in USA

ISBN 978-0-8388-1637-0

15 16 17 18 19 PAH 17 16 15 14 13

Table of Contents

For the Student

Welcome to the world of American history. You are going to read about our country's past. History is filled with exciting stories and interesting people. This book will tell you about some of them. It can also help you practice ways to read and study that you can use in all your classes, not just in history class.

Before you start working in this book, you will need to know how it is put together. Each chapter is arranged into parts that take you along one step at a time. If you follow the directions, you will be able to read and learn the material without any trouble.

To begin with, there are pictures and sometimes maps at the start of each chapter. By studying them, you will get an idea of what you are going to be reading about.

Next, there are a few vocabulary words. This vocabulary section gives meanings and pronunciations for some words that will appear in the chapter. The letters in CAPITALS are parts of the word which are accented, or said the loudest:

example = eg-ZAM-pul

Turn next to the chapter story. At the beginning are two or three questions, just beneath the title. These give you some hints about the main ideas and help you start thinking *before* you read. Keep these questions in mind, and look for the answers as you read.

Some words in the chapter story are printed in heavy black type called **boldface.** These are the words from the vocabulary page. Some other words and names are printed in *italics*. That is a signal to look at the right-hand column of the page if you need help in pronouncing them.

One more thing to look for is a black dot ●. Most chapters are divided into sections, with a dot to show that a main section has come to an end. That should be your signal to stop and think back over the paragraphs in that section. Try to tell yourself the main ideas that were built up. Ask yourself WHAT happened, WHO did it, and WHY. A quick review like this helps you take the facts and ideas from a book and put them into your own words. That is the best way of all to study.

At the end of each chapter you will find exercises to do. Don't think of these as a test. They are designed to help you review the most important facts and ideas in the chapter. As you work along through the book, think carefully about what you are reading. It will help you to do the exercises without having to look back at the chapter.

Exercise A always deals with the main ideas. Ideas are even more important than facts. If you know the main ideas of a story, you understand its meaning. For example, it is just as important to know *why* Columbus came to America as it is to know *when* he came (1492).

Exercise C or D is a vocabulary review. This exercise should be easy. It is designed to help you strengthen and build your vocabulary by giving you extra practice with the words from the first page of the chapter. You will see some of those words again and again in later parts of the book. The last exercise in each chapter is called "Think About and Discuss in Class." Here, you and your classmates can begin to relate the past to the present and to your own lives. You can look for the lessons that history can teach us. Why do wars start? Why do people starve? How can the world be made a happier place to live in?

History teaches us lessons, and it is fun to read. You'll enjoy the stories about the many different kinds of people who live in our country. You'll also ride rockets to outer space with our astronauts. Pick out your favorite subjects and talk about them in class.

As you turn these pages, you will find yourself reading faster and faster. Keep it up! Within a short time, you will be moving easily through this book. It will help make you a better reader and a better student.

Senator Joseph McCarthy accused people of being "disloyal" on the basis of very little or no evidence.

Getting Ready for Chapter One

Here are six vocabulary words that are used in the story about the Eisenhower years. Study these definitions so you will know what each word means when you see it in your reading.

conspiracy   (kon-SPIH-rih-see) Secret agreement or plot to do something wrong — usually by a group of people.

denounce   (dee-NOUNSS) To accuse someone or something in public of being wrong or bad.

summit
conference   (SUM-it KON-frenss) Summit means the top. A summit conference is a meeting of top leaders.

cautious   (KAW-shuss) Very careful; always thinking ahead about risk or danger.

fraud   (FRAWD) Trickery; pretending something is what it really is not.

capitalism   (CAP-ih-tul-IZM) Ownership of business and industry by private citizens instead of by government.

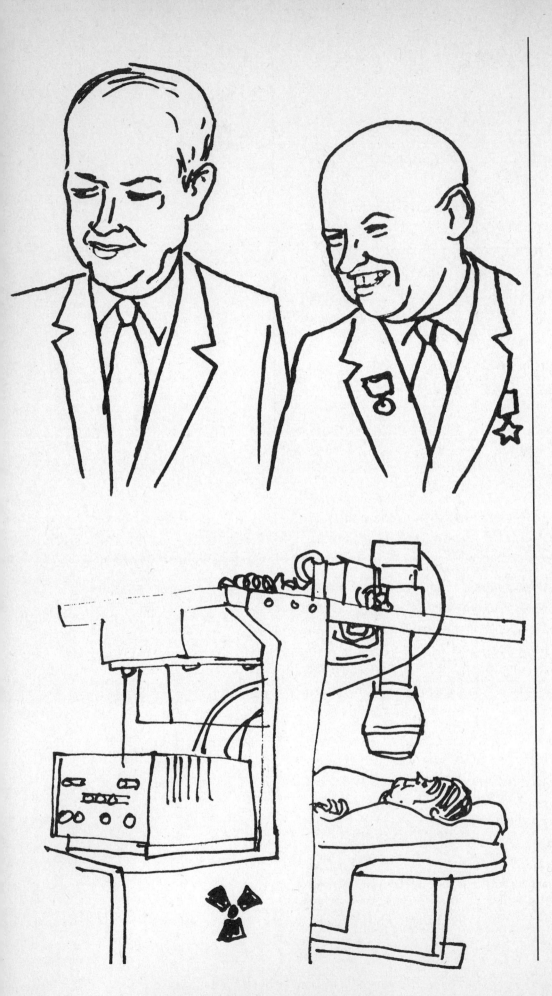

Soviet Premier Khrushchev visited the
United States in 1959 and met with
President Eisenhower.

Atomic energy is used not only in
weapons. It can be used in peaceful
ways too, as in medicine.

The Eisenhower Years

What is McCarthyism?
How did President Eisenhower work for peace?

"I Like Ike!" Americans wore those buttons during the election of 1952.

General Dwight (Ike) Eisenhower was an American hero. He had led our armies to victory in Europe in World War II. He easily won the presidential election. ●

During the 1950s many Americans were worried about communism. The Cold War between the Soviet Union* and the United States was worse. Fear of communism was growing. A Republican senator from Wisconsin, Joseph McCarthy, took *advantage* of this fear.

ad-VAN-tij

McCarthy said that Democrats in the government had spent twenty years in a **conspiracy** to turn this country over to the Soviets. He said that there were "communists" working in the government, in business, education, the arts — everywhere — and that they were plotting to overthrow the American government.

McCarthy was a *dramatic* speaker. He waved papers that he said were lists of people who were communists; he **denounced** people who were famous as well as people who were unknown to the public. He frightened those he accused as well as those who were only listening to his charges. He *ruined* the careers and *reputations* of thousands of people.

druh-MA-tik

ROO-ind
reh-pyoo-TAY-shunz

Finally a Senate committee investigated some of McCarthy's charges and found that they were "a **fraud** . . . on the Senate of the United States and on the American people. They represent perhaps the most serious campaign of half-truth and untruth in the history of the Republic." For example, after investigation, not one of the State Department members McCarthy accused was found guilty of being a communist. ●

The feelings of *suspicion* that McCarthy caused lasted for years. People were afraid to speak out if they disagreed with government policy. They were afraid to sign petitions, or even to *associate* with people whose ideas or opinions were different. They were afraid that if they did these things, they themselves might be called communists

suh-SPIH-shun

uh-SOW-see-ayt

*In 1922 the Union of Soviet Socialist Republics (U.S.S.R.) or Soviet Union for short, became the correct name for the country formerly known as Russia. However, the names Russia and Russians continued in use because the Russian Republic was by far the largest part of the nation. Until recent times, Russia and the Soviet Union meant the same thing.

and might lose their jobs. McCarthy's effect is still felt today. "McCarthyism" means accusing people, without much evidence or proof, of believing things that go against government policies.

While McCarthy was raging about communism in America, President Eisenhower was thinking about foreign policy. He had been a great general, but he hated war. As president, he worked hard for peace. He was especially interested in the problem of atomic energy. Both the United States and the Soviet Union knew how to make weapons using atomic energy. They both had a new bomb even more powerful than the atomic bomb — the hydrogen bomb. There were no plans for peaceful uses of this force, however. ●

In 1953 Eisenhower spoke at the United Nations. He had an idea that he called Atoms for Peace. He said that the Soviet Union and the United States should each give nuclear materials to an international group to develop new ways of using atomic energy, such as making electricity. He thought this would be a good step toward world peace.

At first, the Soviets listened to the plan, but they did not agree. Some Americans were also against it, even though Eisenhower thought his idea was important. The world's first nuclear power plant was built in 1954. Soon the International Atomic Energy Commission was formed to make the peaceful use of atomic energy available to over eighty nations.

Joseph Stalin, the head of the government in the Soviet Union, died in 1953. The new Soviet leaders were friendlier to the United States than Stalin had been. In 1955 they met with Eisenhower for a **summit conference** in Geneva, Switzerland.

At the Geneva conference, Eisenhower offered a peace plan. He said that the Soviet Union and the United States should be friends again. They would not hide military secrets from each other. Under Eisenhower's plan, there would be "open skies" over both the Soviet Union and the United States. Each side could send airplanes over the other's territory. The pilots of the planes would inspect military posts and airfields. They would take pictures with powerful, long-range cameras. In that way, each country would know if the other was preparing for war.

But the new head of the Soviet government, *Nikita Khrushchev,* did not like this idea. He was friendly to Eisenhower, but he still believed that communism should be the form of government everywhere. He knew that America wanted **capitalism** throughout the world. He was **cautious** and did not want to become too close to America. And so the Cold War continued. ●

nih-KEE-tuh
KROOS-chef

In 1959 Eisenhower invited Khrushchev to visit the United States. The Soviet leader accepted the invitation. He traveled around the

4

country. He ate hot dogs and talked to Americans everywhere. He even asked to see Disneyland. He had friendly talks with Eisenhower. A new feeling of warmth developed between the two powerful nations. But there was still trouble in places like Germany, Egypt, and China. The Soviets and Americans had a lot to discuss. A new summit conference to talk about world peace was planned for 1960 in Paris.

But these talks were never held. Just before they began, an American U-2 spy plane flew high over the Soviet Union. We were afraid the Soviets might be hiding something. We wanted to check. Soviet gunners brought the plane down. The pilot was unhurt. He admitted he was a U.S. spy and was sent to a Soviet prison.

Khrushchev was very angry. He asked Eisenhower why the spy plane had been sent. At first, Eisenhower said that the plane had become lost while it was studying the weather. Then he admitted that the pilot was really spying and taking pictures of Soviet nuclear plants. Khrushchev felt that the Americans had not played fair. He called off the peace talks. In later years many other peace talks were held. The Soviet Union and the United States continued trying to learn how to deal with each other.

Eisenhower was a very popular president. He did not end the Cold War, but he did keep *communication* open between the United States and the Soviet Union. His cautious attitudes worked well in keeping America out of war at an important time. He will be remembered as a loved and respected leader.

kum-yoon-ih-KAY-shun

Answer these to review the main ideas.

A.

1. What did Senator McCarthy say the "communists" in America were

   doing? _____

_____

2. What did the Senate Committee find out when they looked into

   McCarthy's accusations? _____

_____

3. What is McCarthyism? _____

_____

4. What was the "Atoms for Peace" program? _____

_____

5

5. What peace plan did Eisenhower offer at the Geneva Conference?

_____

6. Why did we send U-2 planes to fly over the Soviet Union? _____

_____

Circle the right answer to finish each sentence.

B.

1. McCarthy took advantage of America's

   a. ideas about the   b. fear of   c. love of Wisconsin
      arts   communism

2. McCarthy was a

   a. boring speaker   b. truthful speaker   c. dramatic speaker

3. Eisenhower wanted atomic energy to be used for

   a. peaceful   b. making war   c. blowing up the
      purposes   Soviet Union

4. A summit conference was held in Geneva in

   a. 1954   b. 1955   c. 1975

5. Eisenhower spoke about his "Atoms for Peace" program at

   a. the Geneva   b. the United   c. the White House
      Conference   Nations

Circle True or False.

C.

T F 1. Most Americans liked Joseph McCarthy.

T F 2. McCarthy had proof that many people in the American government were communists.

T F 3. Joseph Stalin was not as friendly to the United States as Khrushchev was.

T F 4. Under Eisenhower's "open skies" plan, the United States and the Soviet Union would be able to fly over each other's territory.

T F 5. Khrushchev refused to visit the United States.

T F 6. The United States sent a plane to spy over the Soviet Union.

Choose one of these words to fit each sentence below.

cautious   conspiracy   fraud
denounced   summit conference   capitalism

1. When top leaders of several countries meet, they are holding a

_____ .

2. The two strangers were arrested for organizing a _____
   to kill the queen.

3. A Senate committee _____ McCarthy as a liar.

4. Eisenhower was very _____ in dealing with the Soviet
   Union because he did not want to start a nuclear war.

5. He was charged with _____ for selling bonds that were
   worthless.

6. Under _____, business and industry are owned by
   private citizens instead of the government.

Think about and discuss in class.

Why did so few Americans stand up to McCarthy at first? _____

_____

_____

Do you think it was a wise thing for the United States to send a spy plane
over the Soviet Union? Why or why not? Do you think it was all right for

President Eisenhower to lie to the Soviets? Explain. _____

_____

_____

_____

_____

What can we do to keep countries from starting a nuclear war? _____

_____

_____

_____

_____

D.

E.

7

Jim Crow laws discriminated against Blacks. For example, Blacks had to drink at separate water fountains.

Federal troops protected the few Black students who were going to a white school in Little Rock, Arkansas.

Blacks "sat-in" at lunch counters where they were refused service.

Getting Ready for Chapter Two

2

Here are eight vocabulary words that are used in the first part of the story about the fight for civil rights. Study these definitions so you will know what each word means when you see it in your reading.

create   (kree-AYT) To make; to bring into existence.

civil rights   (cih-vil RITES) The rights given to all Americans by the Constitution — especially equality of treatment in employment, education, housing, and public services.

prejudice   (PREH-joo-diss) A strong feeling against something or someone which is not based on facts or knowledge.

discriminate   (dis-KRIH-mih-nayt) To treat one thing or person differently from the way you treat another; usually to treat unfairly.

facilities   (fuh-SIL-ih-teez) Things meant to be used for a particular purpose — like a building or machinery.

segregation   (seh-gruh-GAY-shun) Separating or isolating one group from a larger group.

integration   (in-tuh-GRAY-shun) Blending or mixing two separate groups into one whole group; uniting.

stereotype   (STER-ee-uh-type) A person or a thing that people *think* is what all such people or things are like, but which is not based on what the person or thing is *really* like.

The Fight for Civil Rights I

What does "Jim Crow" mean?
Why was 1954 an important year for all Americans?

Americans believe that all who obey the law should be free. Everyone should also be treated fairly.

The Declaration of Independence says that "all men are **created** equal" and that everyone has the right to "life, liberty, and the *pursuit* of happiness." The Bill of Rights of the Constitution spells out and *guarantees* the **civil rights** of all citizens. But Black people in America do not have complete freedom and equality.

pur-SOOT

gar-un-TEEZ

The ancestors of most Black Americans were brought here as prisoners and forced to be slaves. Blacks in the southern states were slaves until the end of the Civil War. People were bought and sold the way horses were. They did not have any of the rights that their white owners had.

After the Civil War, all slaves were freed. Congress amended, or changed, the Constitution to say that slavery was against the law, and that Blacks were full citizens of their states and of the nation. As citizens, they had the right to vote. Now, at least according to the written law, they had the civil rights that should have been theirs all along.

But many white people, especially in the southern states, were not happy about this new equality. They passed their own state laws to keep Blacks from having the same freedom that white people have. These laws came to be known as Jim Crow laws.*

Jim Crow laws **discriminated** against Blacks. They forced Blacks to ride in *separate* train cars, to use separate waiting rooms, and to sit in the backs of buses. According to these laws, Black people could not go to school with whites. They had to go to separate schools. They could not use "white" playgrounds and had to drink from separate drinking fountains! Much more money was spent on services for whites than for Blacks. Blacks were treated as second-class citizens. ●

SEP-rit

Blacks continued to try to vote in spite of the unfair laws. At this time the Ku Klux Klan was formed to frighten Blacks. Many people were lynched (hanged until dead) simply because they were Black. In 1896, a Black man named Homer *Plessy* went to court to fight for the right to ride in the same train car with whites. He took his case all the way to the Supreme Court, the highest court in the land.

PLESS-ee

*The name Jim Crow came from a **stereotyped** Black character in a song-and-dance act performed in the nineteenth century.

The Supreme Court decides on a case by thinking about whether the law follows what the Constitution says. In the Plessy case, the Court said that it was all right for a state to make a law which separated Blacks and whites on trains. Segregation was legal as long as the services for Blacks were as good as the services for whites.

This decision came to be known as the "separate but equal" decision. It remained in effect for fifty-eight years. The southern states were pleased with the Court's decision. By 1910 all the former Confederate states had passed laws that kept most Blacks from voting.

Blacks began to build organizations to fight these unfair laws. In 1901, the NAACP (National Association for the Advancement of Colored People) was formed. In 1911, the National Urban League began. And in 1939 the Defense Fund of the NAACP was started. Its first director was Thurgood Marshall, who later was appointed the first Black Supreme Court justice.

In the 1940s, President Franklin *Roosevelt* made some important changes. When a march on Washington, D.C., protesting discrimination in the armed forces, was about to happen, Roosevelt outlawed **segregation** in federal offices and began **integration** of the armed forces. He wrote orders saying that companies doing business with the government had to hire Blacks as well as whites. While Harry Truman was president, he formed a Commission on Civil Rights, which worked for an end to all segregation. Some white Americans were beginning to see the unfairness of how Blacks were treated. ●

ROH-ze-velt

In 1954, during Eisenhower's first term as president, the Supreme Court made a very important ruling. The Court agreed to hear a civil rights case between a Black man named Oliver Brown and the school board of *Topeka*, Kansas. Brown wanted his eight-year-old daughter to attend a white school. The white school was close to her home, while the Black school was so far away that the little girl had to walk twenty-one blocks through heavy traffic just to get a bus to take her there. The Topeka school board would not allow her to go to the white school. Brown sued the board for showing **prejudice**.

tuh-PEE-kuh

Chief Justice Earl Warren and the Supreme Court studied the *Brown v. (Topeka) Board of Education* case very carefully. They saw that according to the old Plessy ruling, it was legal for the child to go to an all-Black school, as long as the Black school was as good as the white school — "separate, but equal." They talked about what segregation means to a Black child. They thought about the Fourteenth Amendment to the Constitution, which guarantees "equal protection of the laws" to all Americans. The Court thought that according to this Amendment, everyone, Black and white, has the right to go to *any* school.

So the Supreme Court in 1954 decided that "separate but equal" **facilities**, created by whites to keep Blacks down, are unequal simply because they are separate. Every member of the Court, including three southerners, agreed that public schools could not be segregated. They said it was not fair or right.

This decision was important for the whole country. In 1955, the Court ordered all states to begin to integrate their schools. Some states obeyed. In Baltimore, Maryland, and St. Louis, *Missouri*, Black students and white students went to school together for the first time, but many southern states hung back.

mih-ZUR-ee

In Little Rock, *Arkansas*, the governor ordered the National Guard to stop a few Black students from going to a white school. President Eisenhower sent federal troops to protect the students. The next year, the governor ordered the public schools in Little Rock to be closed. Other states tried this and other ways to *avoid* school integration. One excuse used for keeping segregation was that Blacks and whites usually lived in separate communities and it would be very expensive to send pupils of either race to a distant location for school. But often, white communities had more money than Black communities and could vote more funds for better paid teachers and better schools. There were big battles over integration, both in court and at the schools themselves. Even today, almost forty years after the *Brown* court case, many schools have not been integrated. ●

AR-kun-saw

uh-VOYD

But the fight for integration of schools slowly began to bring down the walls of segregation that surrounded Blacks. Blacks pushed for the right to use any hotel, restaurant, or other service. They demanded an end to state laws which kept them from voting.

The fight for Black civil rights has been a long and difficult one. It will probably continue for many years. But the *Brown v. Board of Education* Court ruling in 1954 was an important start toward an integrated America.

Answer these to review the main ideas.

A.

1. According to the Constitution, what basic rights are all Americans

   entitled to? _____

   _____

2. After the Civil War, how did white people try to keep Blacks from

   having the freedom given to them by law? _____

   _____

   _____

3. What did the Supreme Court rule in the *Plessy* case? _____

_____

_____

4. What did the Supreme Court rule in the *Brown v. Board of Education*

case? _____

_____

5. Why was the *Brown v. Board of Education* case important for both

Blacks and whites? _____

_____

Circle True or False.   **B.**

T   F   1. In the *Plessy* case, the Supreme Court ruled that Blacks and
           whites could have separate but equal services.

T   F   2. The Declaration of Independence guarantees us our civil
           rights.

T   F   3. Blacks originally came to America as pilgrims.

T   F   4. Jim Crow laws were passed to give Blacks more equality.

T   F   5. President Franklin Roosevelt said Blacks did not have the
           training to get jobs in industry.

Circle the right answer to finish each sentence.   **C.**

1. The Supreme Court makes rulings on its cases according to

   a. the president   b. the Constitution   c. the Chief Justice

2. Jim Crow means

   a. segregation   b. integration   c. congregation

3. The Chief Justice of the Supreme Court in the *Brown v. Board of
   Education* case was

   a. Homer Plessy   b. Oliver Brown   c. Earl Warren

4. The Supreme Court decided that "separate but equal" facilities are unequal simply because

    a. they are separate   b. they cost a lot to build   c. Blacks don't take pride in American ideals

5. The Fourteenth Amendment to the Constitution says Americans have

    a. "equal protection of the laws"   b. "separate protection"   c. "no protection"

Choose one of these words to fit each sentence below.

D.

create	segregation	civil rights
prejudice	discriminate	facilities
integration	stereotype	

1. In the 1954 Supreme Court decision, all the Court members agreed that _____ of public schools is wrong.

2. President Roosevelt began _____ of the armed forces.

3. Even though Blacks and whites have equal rights according to the law, many people still _____ against Blacks.

4. Before 1954, Blacks had to go to segregated schools and use many other _____ that were separate from whites.

5. To dislike other people just because they look different from us is to be _____d against them.

6. The Declaration of Independence tells us that all people, regardless of race or color, are _____d equal.

7. She fits the _____ of a scientist — pale, thin, near-sighted, and serious.

8. _____ _____ is a subject of importance to all Americans.

Think about and discuss in class.

The v. in *Brown v. Board of Education* means *versus*. What does that mean? (If you need to, you may use the dictionary.) _____

_____

Do you know the Pledge of Allegiance to the flag? What does it mean? How does it end? _____

_____

Why do you think people become prejudiced against a group because of its skin color or religion? What can be done to fight this kind of prejudice? _____

_____

_____

E.

Fifty thousand Blacks and whites had a nonviolent demonstration for voting rights in Selma, Alabama. Police tried to stop it by beating demonstrators and using tear gas.

After the Voting Rights Bill was passed in 1965 Blacks could register to vote.

Rosa Parks, a Black woman, was arrested for refusing to get up and give her seat to a white man.

Getting Ready for Chapter Three

3

Here are seven vocabulary words that are used in the continuing story about the fight for civil rights. Study these definitions so you will know what each word means when you see it in your reading.

boycott
(BOY-kot) Refusing to deal with, or buy goods from, a person or a business as a protest against them.

resistance
(ree-ZISS-tunss) Not going along with something; opposing something.

nonviolent
(non-VY-uh-lunt) Without using violence (physical force).

terrorize
(TER-ur-eyes) To create fear by violence or threat.

demonstra-tion
(dem-un-STRAY-shun) A parade or gathering of people to show feelings about a public issue.

sit-in
(SIT-in) A group of people sitting in a building and refusing to move or leave in order to protest against something.

tear gas
(TEER-gas) A gas that stings and blinds people's eyes with tears — used to stop demonstrations.

The Fight for Civil Rights II

Why is Rosa Parks well known?
What kind of protest did Martin Luther King, Jr., believe in?

It was a cold evening in December 1955. Rosa Parks was very tired. She had been sewing and fitting dresses all day long at a department store in Montgomery, Alabama. Mrs. Parks was waiting for a city bus to come so she could get home.

When the bus finally came, Mrs. Parks paid her fare and took a seat. How good it felt after a long day's work! She settled back to rest. More people boarded the bus, but there were not enough seats for everyone. Some white people were standing in the *aisle*.

EYE-ul

The bus driver told Mrs. Parks to get up. A man was waiting to take Mrs. Parks' seat. Mrs. Parks was Black. The man was white.

The law in the city of Montgomery said that if a bus filled up, Blacks must give up their seats to whites and move back in the aisle. That meant Mrs. Parks would have to stand in the back of the bus.

Rosa Parks was a quiet, middle-aged woman. She was not afraid. Since the Supreme Court ruling against segregation in public schools, Blacks were beginning to feel more strongly about demanding their rights. Mrs. Parks decided to disobey the law. She remained in her seat. The white bus driver again told Mrs. Parks to move. Other Blacks were moving back in the aisle to obey the law.

Mrs. Parks quietly refused. She remembered what the Supreme Court had ruled the year before in the *Brown v. Board of Education* case. Schools must be integrated. Then why not buses and all the other things that were segregated?

The bus driver got off the bus and found a policeman. The policeman arrested Mrs. Parks. She was charged with breaking the Montgomery law. ●

The story of Mrs. Parks' arrest spread all over the city. Many Black people had been forced to give their bus seats to whites, and they thought Mrs. Parks had done the right thing. Black leaders in Montgomery organized a **boycott** of the city buses. Beginning the day of Mrs. Parks' trial, Blacks would not ride on the buses. They planned to stay off the buses until they had the same rights on them as whites did.

The leader of the boycott was a twenty-six-year-old Black minister named Martin Luther King, Jr. King was just beginning his ministry in Montgomery and was loyal to the Black civil rights cause. He believed in taking direct action to improve the conditions of Black life, but he did not believe that violence was a good way to change things.

He preached that Blacks should use peaceful **resistance** to protest unfair conditions.

Mrs. Parks was fined $14 by a Montgomery judge for breaking the law. Her lawyers took the case to a higher court. Meanwhile the city's Blacks stayed off the buses. They walked to work, took taxicabs, or rode in car pools that they organized. Some even rode mules.

The boycott worked very well. Blacks had used the buses more than whites. Now the buses were almost empty. The bus company lost thousands of dollars every day. Montgomery's stores lost business, too, because it was hard for people to get there. Many workers lost their jobs.

Angry whites demanded an end to the boycott. White gangs began to **terrorize** Blacks. King and other Black leaders were put in jail, but the boycott continued.

In January 1956, someone threw a bomb at Dr. King's house. King was at church, but his wife, Coretta, and their baby were there. Both were unhurt, but the house was damaged.

Rosa Parks took her case all the way to the United States Supreme Court. In November 1956, the Court ruled that segregation in public transportation was illegal. This was a great victory for the Montgomery bus boycott and for Blacks all over the United States. It encouraged **demonstrations** in other cities. The idea of peaceful resistance was catching on. In 1960 in Greensboro, North Carolina, four Black college students ordered coffee at a dime-store lunch counter. The clerk refused to serve them. They remained there quietly, not demanding anything, but refusing to leave, even when the manager called the police to get them out. ●

People across the country were inspired by the bravery of these students. **Sit-ins** spread throughout the southern states. Nonviolent protest helped change the law: restaurants in at least eight states were desegregated as a direct result of the sit-ins.

Martin Luther King, Jr., continued to be a leader of the **nonviolent** civil rights movement through the early 1960s. Many whites responded to the movement with violence. In 1963, for example, dynamite explosions were set off at a civil rights headquarters. However, King said that even though some whites were using violence in their fight against integration, Blacks should keep on using nonviolence. Later that year he led the peaceful March on Washington for Jobs and Freedom, in which he spoke to over 200,000 demonstrators about his dream of freedom and equality for all.

In 1964 Congress passed the Civil Rights Act, which said discrimination in public facilities was against the law. Blacks had a legal right to go to the same restaurants, theaters, hotels, and other public places that whites went to. Then in 1965 King led a nonviolent demonstration for voting rights in Selma, Alabama. Law officers tried to stop the demonstration by beating the demonstrators and using **tear gas**. In protest, 50,000 people, both black and white, marched fifty miles to Montgomery, Alabama. Their demands were met, for President Johnson signed the Voting Rights Bill in 1965. This bill said that all Blacks must have the full rights of American citizens. In 1968 the Fair Housing Act said that no one can refuse to sell a house to someone because of the person's race or color.

These civil rights bills were important steps. But by this time many people had become impatient with nonviolent tactics and with going through the courts. Too many times Blacks had had to suffer acts of violence without fighting back. Court battles took a lot of time and money, and too many times the passing of laws did not really change the way Blacks lived.

In the late sixties, the centuries of Black anger at injustice began to be expressed by riots in many large cities and by violent protest marches. In 1968 Martin Luther King, Jr., was planning a Poor People's Campaign. Hundreds of thousands of poor Blacks and whites were going to demonstrate against unemployment, bad housing, and other unfair conditions.

In the middle of the planning, Dr. King flew to Memphis, Tennessee, to lead a demonstration of sanitation workers who were on strike. He was shot and killed while he was in his motel by James Earl Ray. The shock and the shame of his murder is still remembered by millions of Americans.

Answer these questions to review the main ideas.

A.

1. What happened when Rosa Parks refused to give up her seat on the

   bus? _____

   _____

   _____

2. What did Martin Luther King, Jr., think about violence? _____

   _____

3. Why did the Montgomery bus boycott work? _____

   _____

4. Why did four college students in North Carolina stage a sit-in? _____

   _____

20

5. Why did sit-ins work? _____

_____

6. What civil rights laws did Congress pass in 1964 and 1965? _____

_____

Circle the right answer to finish each sentence.

B.

1. Rosa Parks was ordered to give up her seat because

   a. the bus driver   b. a white man   c. she was only
      didn't like her   wanted her seat   going a short way

2. The law said that if a bus filled up

   a. all Blacks should   b. older people   c. Blacks should
      get off   should sit and   move to the back
                                  younger ones   of the bus
                                  should stand

3. Martin Luther King, Jr., believed that

   a. Blacks were   b. the Black situa-   c. direct but peace-
      lucky to be   tion in America   ful action should
      allowed on buses   was hopeless   be taken to
                                                          improve condi-
                                                          tions for Blacks

4. The Montgomery bus boycott

   a. helped business   b, hurt business   c. made no
                                                          difference

5. Sit-ins helped to

   a. desegregate   b. stop the bus   c. frighten Blacks
      restaurants   boycott

Circle True or False.

C.

T F   1. The city laws of Montgomery said that if a bus filled up, men
          had to give their seats to women and move to the back of the
          bus.

T F   2. The bus driver told Mrs. Parks to move to another seat.

T F   3. The bus boycott caused many stores to lose business because
          people did not go downtown.

T F 4. The Supreme Court ruled that Montgomery's busing law was unfair.

T F 5. Dr. King led a march on Washington for states' rights.

Choose one of these words to fit each sentence below.

boycott   nonviolent   demonstration   tear gas

resistance   terrorize   sit-in

1. If people get together and refuse to buy someone's goods or go to a particular place, they are organizing a _____.

2. If protesters are _____ they are not using force or weapons.

3. Whites with clubs and other weapons _____d the Black protesters.

4. People at the _____ were marching through the streets, carrying signs and shouting loudly.

5. Four college students staged a _____ in Greensboro, North Carolina.

6. When the police used _____, the demonstrators covered their eyes and moved back.

7. Martin Luther King, Jr., believed that peaceful _____ to unfair laws was the way to change things.

Think about and discuss in class.

If someone hits you, should you hit back? What else could you do? _____

_____

Many laws have been passed to give Black Americans equal rights as citizens. Yet the struggle goes on. What areas of Black American life can you think of which might not be helped by laws alone? _____

_____

_____

Find something in the library to read about Martin Luther King, Jr. He has become famous all over the world. What kind of person was he? What were his beliefs about how society should be run? What finally happened to Dr. King? _____

_____

_____

Volunteers in the Peace Corps went to other countries to teach more modern methods of farming.

Fidel Castro led a people's revolution which brought communism to Cuba.

Getting Ready for Chapter Four

Here are eight vocabulary words that are used in the story about John F. Kennedy. Study these definitions so you will know what each word means when you see it in your reading.

missile
(MISS-il) Any weapon that is fired, thrown, or dropped on a target.

underdeveloped
(un-dur-dee-VEL-upt) A word used by industrialized countries to describe countries that do not have much industry or technology.

volunteer
(vol-un-TEER) A person who offers, of his or her own free will, to do something.

invade
(in-VAYD) To go into a place with troops, as in a war, in order to take control.

fascist
(FASH-ust) A person who believes in a government run by a dictator who controls what goes on in the country and who will punish or even kill anyone who has different ideas.

investments
(in-VEST-muntz) Money put into property or business in order to make more money

exiles
(EK-siles) People who have left a country, sometimes by force, because they do not agree with its government.

launch
(LAWNCH) To start; to set out, as on the sea.

John F. Kennedy was a popular president who started the Peace Corps.

President John F. Kennedy

Why was November 22, 1963, a dark day in American history?
What was the Cuban **missile** crisis?

November 22, 1963 was a day most adult Americans will never forget. It was the day that President John F. Kennedy was assassinated. Kennedy was a young president who was popular with millions of people in America and around the world. Many people had thought that Kennedy's leadership made peace and prosperity for all people more likely.

John Fitzgerald Kennedy was born in Brookline, Massachusetts, in 1917. He was the second son in a family of nine children. Jack, as he was called, went to private schools and then Harvard College, where he took many courses in government and history.

After college, Kennedy joined the navy. In 1943, during World War II, his torpedo boat was rammed by a Japanese destroyer. Although he was injured, Kennedy swam three miles to shore, carrying another *wounded* sailor with him. He was a hero, winning several medals for his bravery.

WOON-did

When the war ended, Kennedy went into politics. First he was elected a Democratic representative and then a senator from Massachusetts. He fought for things like better public housing and social security programs. By 1960, when he decided to run for president, he was well known in the Democratic party.

Kennedy ran against a Republican, Richard Nixon. Some people thought Kennedy could not win because he was a Roman Catholic. Only one Catholic had run for president before, and he had lost. But in 1960 Americans elected Kennedy in a close race. ●

At his inauguration, Kennedy spoke of protecting human rights everywhere. He also told Americans that they should love and be proud of their country. He asked them to help this nation as much as they could. He said, "And so, my fellow Americans, ask not what your country can do for you — ask what you can do for your country."

The new president was in favor of the Black struggle for equality. He came to the aid of a Black student who wanted to attend the University of Mississippi. James Meredith could not get in because of his color. The governor of Mississippi himself was blocking Meredith's entrance to school. Kennedy sent federal troops and police to Mississippi. They protected Meredith from the mobs who did not want him at the university. They even went with him to classes in order to make sure that he was safe. The *soldiers* protected him until he was graduated. Meredith's action helped Blacks enter universities all over the country. ●

SOLE-jers

To improve the way people lived in **underdeveloped** countries around the world, Kennedy started the Peace *Corps*. This group sent **volunteer** doctors, nurses, teachers, *engineers*, and farmers to foreign countries to teach and help people who needed them. The Peace Corps is still working today.

KOR
en-jin-EERZ

The Cold War with the Soviet Union went on, even though Kennedy's first speech had talked of his hopes for peace. The two countries were both making powerful atomic weapons. Each country feared and hated the other. This atomic arms race was very dangerous. It could easily lead to a nuclear war. In a nuclear war entire civilizations would be destroyed. ●

In 1959, Cuba, a small Caribbean nation ninety miles south of Florida, had a revolution led mostly by peasants. They overthrew the **fascist** dictator. The leader of the revolution, *Fidel Castro*, became the new president. Castro was a communist who was sympathetic to the Soviet Union, and the Soviets supported the Cuban revolution. The U.S. Congress, hoping that the Cuban revolution would fail, stopped buying sugar from them. Sugar was Cuba's main crop and the thing they exported most. The Cubans lost a lot of money. Cuba then took over millions of dollars worth of American **investments** in Cuba.

fee-DELL CAS-tro

Cubans who did not like the changes in their country came to America. They planned to return and **invade** Cuba and try to get rid of Castro. These **exiles** wanted help from us.

Kennedy did not want communism to spread to other Latin American countries. But he also did not want to risk a war between the Soviet Union and the United States. So he made a deal with the exiles. He gave them American weapons and American ships, but no troops to back them up. About 1500 Cuban **exiles** left from Florida to **launch** an attack on Cuba. They were quickly driven back by the Cuban army at the Bay of Pigs. The exiles begged the United States to supply them with airplanes and troops, but the Soviets warned that if America sent its forces to Cuba, they would send troops to fight them. Kennedy did not want to risk war. He would not give the exiles more help. The exiles were defeated.

The next move the Soviets made was a surprise. They set up missiles in Cuba that were aimed at the United States. Since America is so close to Cuba, these missiles could easily have hit our country. Kennedy *immediately* warned Soviet Premier Khrushchev that he must remove all the missiles from Cuba. Kennedy said the United States would block any more shipments.

ih-MEED-ee-ut-lee

The Soviets replied that they would **launch** an attack if the Americans tried to stop their ships. Americans were afraid that we might have a nuclear war. Khrushchev realized how serious we were, and he

27

ordered the missiles removed. The Cuban missile crisis was over. The Soviets, like Kennedy, did not want to risk war. ●

Kennedy, unfortunately, was not able to finish his first term in office. In the third year of his presidency, he and his wife were visiting Dallas, Texas. They were riding in an open automobile, waving to an *enthusiastic* crowd. Suddenly a shot rang out, and Kennedy slumped in his seat. He was killed by a man named Lee Harvey Oswald. Kennedy's sudden death was a tragedy which filled the world with grief. Americans felt that they had lost a special leader and friend.

en-thoo-zee-AS-tik

Answer these to review the main ideas.

A.

1. How did John F. Kennedy become a war hero? _____

_____

_____

2. What is the Peace Corps? _____

_____

3. What compromise did Kennedy make with the Cuban exiles? _____

_____

_____

4. What was the Cuban missile crisis? _____

_____

_____

5. What happened in Dallas, Texas, on November 22, 1963? _____

_____

Circle the right answer to finish each sentence.

B.

1. The man who shot President Kennedy was

   a. Fidel Castro   b. Lee Harvey   c. James Meredith
                              Oswald

2. The Cuban exiles were defeated by Castro's troops at

   a. Havana   b. Puerto Rico   c. the Bay of Pigs

3. Kennedy's home state was

   a. Georgia   b. California   c. Massachusetts

28

4. The distance between Cuba and the United States is

   a. ninety miles   b. two hundred   c. nine miles

                             miles

5. Kennedy did not send troops to the Bay of Pigs because

   a. we did not have   b. he wanted to win   c. the Soviets
       enough forces   a nuclear war   threatened
                                                            to fight any
                                                             American troops
                                                             sent to Cuba

Circle True or False.   C.

T   F   1. John Kennedy was an only child.

T   F   2. Kennedy's plane was shot down in World War II.

T   F   3. Kennedy believed in less government spending on programs for the poor.

T   F   4. James Meredith was a Black student who wanted to attend the University of Mississippi.

T   F   5. Kennedy threatened to put missiles in Poland if the Soviets left the missiles in Cuba.

Choose one of these words to fit each sentence below.   D.

launch   underdeveloped   invade   fascist

missile   investments   volunteers   exiles

1. Cuba's _____ were angry at the new government.

2. The United States did not want Soviet _____s in Cuba.

3. The Soviets said they would _____ an attack.

4. Many American businesses had _____ in Cuba.

5. The exiles wanted to _____ Cuba.

6. Cuba had a _____ ruler before the revolution.

7. Industrialized countries say that countries without much industry are

_____.

8. The Peace Corps is made up of _____s.

Think about and discuss in class.

Name some other American presidents and important leaders who have been assassinated. Why do you think anyone would want to assassinate a president or other leader? _____

_____

_____

Why do you think some people care about the religious beliefs of the president? _____

_____

Should President Kennedy have sent American troops and planes to help the Cuban exiles fighting at the Bay of Pigs? Why or why not? _____

_____

_____

Do you think we will ever have a nuclear war? Why would any country start a nuclear war, since the whole world could easily be destroyed by it?

_____

_____

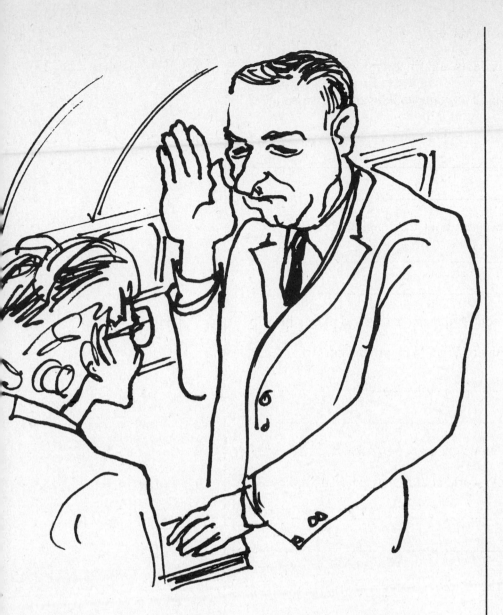

Getting Ready for Chapter Five

5

Here are five vocabulary words that are used in the story of President Lyndon B. Johnson. Study these definitions so you will know what each word means when you see it in your reading.

stunned   (STUND) Completely shocked and surprised; overcome with amazement.

urge   (ERJ) To encourage strongly; to argue in favor of.

poverty   (POV-ur-tee) The condition of being very poor and needy.

parochial   (puh-ROH-kee-ul) Supported by a religious group, such as a church.

vocational   (voh-KAY-shun-ul) Having to do with a kind of work or occupation.

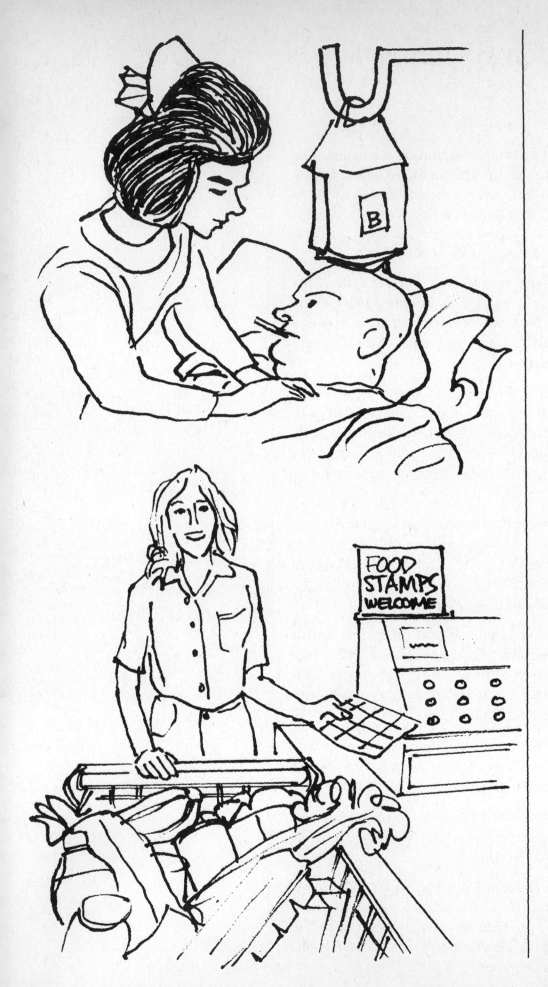

Medicare helps Americans over 65 pay doctors' and hospital bills.

Another program of Johnson's Great Society was food stamps. Low-income people can use the stamps to help buy food.

President Lyndon B. Johnson

What was the Great Society?
What caused Johnson's downfall?

The assassination of President Kennedy **stunned** the nation. But quick action had to be taken so that the United States would have a new leader. When the president dies, the vice president takes over. On November 22, 1963, on board the jet that carried Kennedy's body, vice-president *Lyndon* B. Johnson was sworn in as president. Johnson became president less than two hours after Kennedy's death.

LIN-dun

Johnson knew that the government must keep going in spite of the tragedy. On November 27 he gave a speech in Congress in which he said there should be "an end to the teaching and preaching of hate and violence." Then he said we should finish programs which Kennedy started. "Let us continue!" he **urged**.

The new president seemed very different from the old one. Kennedy had been young and rich, and he was raised and went to school in the Northeast. Johnson was from Texas. He was the son of a rancher. He was older than Kennedy and had a lot of experience in politics. Before he was vice president, he had been a senator for many years.

People wondered how Johnson would handle civil rights programs. He was a southerner, and Blacks in the South were fighting hard for civil rights. One of the first things that Johnson did as president was to urge Congress to pass Kennedy's civil rights bill. It was clear that the southern-born Johnson believed in civil rights for Blacks.

Johnson also showed that he thought a decent life for *all* human beings was important. He called for a fight against **poverty** in this country which would help to turn the United States into what he called a "Great Society." Congress voted one billion dollars to carry out this plan.

He also asked that Congress pass Kennedy's bill lowering taxes, an education bill, and a bill for aid to other countries. Johnson was *popular* in Washington, and he knew how to get laws passed. He carried out Kennedy's unfinished programs as well as programs of his own.

POP-yoo-lur

Most Americans liked Johnson's Great Society programs. In 1964, after he had been president for one year, elections were held. Johnson was reelected to four more years in office. ●

Under Johnson, the federal government spent money to improve public health, education, and welfare. Both public and **parochial** schools got money. The funds were spent in several ways. Much of it went to educating slow learners. Some went to **vocational** education. Federal money also paid for kindergartens and milk programs.

The government did other things to help the poor and needy of all races. For example, it started a food-stamp plan. Low-income families could get stamps. Using some money of their own and food stamps, they could buy food.

One of Johnson's most important *achievements* was the Medicare Bill. This bill helped Americans over 65 to pay doctors' and hospital bills.

uh-CHEEV-muntz

All these programs cost billions of dollars. Some people thought it was a mistake for the government to spend so much. But most people felt the causes were important and that the country could afford to spend the money. ●

President Johnson wanted to improve the way Americans lived. He wanted to be remembered in history as one of our best presidents. But he failed. Why?

The answer is *Vietnam*. Vietnam is a small country in Asia. After years of being ruled by the French, Vietnam was fighting for its independence. America was afraid that a communist government would gain power over the whole country. If this happened in Vietnam, it might happen in other countries in Southeast Asia. Johnson sent American planes and soldiers to Vietnam to stop the communists and to support a government friendly to the West.

vyet-NAHM

You will read more about the Vietnam War later in this book. Johnson did not want to send American soldiers to Vietnam. But he also did not want to be the president who was in power when Vietnam became a communist country. *Gradually*, America became more involved in the war. Johnson sent more troops and began bombing raids. By the end of the war over fifty thousand Americans and one million *Vietnamese* had died. Much of Vietnam was totally destroyed.

GRA-joo-uh-lee

vyet-nah-MEEZ

Many Americans blamed President Johnson for keeping us involved in the Vietnam War. Vietnam made people forget the good things he had done for the country, and Johnson became very unpopular. He decided not to run for reelection in 1968 because many people were against him. The Vietnam War ended Johnson's career in politics, and it caused serious problems for America.

Answer these to review the main ideas.

A.

1. How was President Johnson's background different from Kennedy's?

_____

_____

2. How did President Johnson feel about civil rights? _____

_____

3. What did Johnson's Great Society do for the American people?

_____

_____

4. What is Medicare? _____

_____

5. Why did President Johnson become unpopular? _____

_____

Circle the right answer to finish each sentence.

B.

1. Lyndon Johnson took the oath as president when he was

   a. on a jet   b. in Congress   c. on a ranch

2. Johnson was not as well educated as Kennedy, but he

   a. was richer   b. was smarter   c. had more
                                                       political
                                                       experience

3. Johnson wanted federal funds to be spent on

   a. space trips   b. health and   c. the 1964 election
                                    education
                                    improvements

4. Johnson was blamed for

   a. being against   b. starting the   c. getting America
      civil rights   Great Society   into a war

5. Johnson did not run for reelection in 1968 because

   a. he wanted to   b. public feeling   c. he had already
      work on his   was against   served two
      ranch   him   terms

Circle True or False.

T F 1. Johnson was against civil rights for Blacks.

T F 2. Johnson helped to pass many of Kennedy's programs in Congress.

T F 3. If an American president is killed, a new president is elected one year later.

T F 4. The Great Society programs helped people in foreign countries.

T F 5. Johnson became very unpopular after he sent Americans to fight in Vietnam.

Choose one of these words to fit each sentence below.

stunned   poverty   parochial

urge   vocational

1. Johnson wanted to spend government money on programs to fight

_____.

2. The nation was _____ at the news of Kennedy's death.

3. Was it legal to use federal funds to support _____

schools?

4. The senator will _____ that Congress pass that bill.

5. They learned to repair engines in _____ school.

Think about and discuss in class.

Was Lyndon Johnson a good president? What makes a good president?

_____

_____

_____

President Johnson was good at politics. What do politicians do? _____

_____

_____

_____

Where does the money to run your school come from? Do the state and

federal governments help?_____

_____

_____

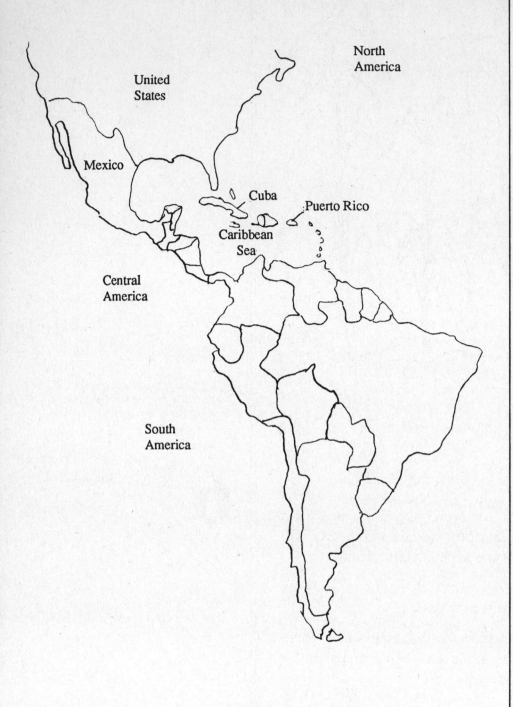

North
America

United
States

Mexico

Cuba

Puerto Rico

Caribbean
Sea

Central
America

South
America

In the past, many Spanish-speaking
Americans came to the United States
from Mexico, Cuba, and Puerto Rico.
Now they also come from many
different countries in Central and South
America.

Many Chicanos do farm work in California and other parts of the Southwest. Their wages are very low.

Getting Ready for Chapter Six

6

Here are seven vocabulary words that are used in the story about Spanish-speaking Americans. Study these definitions so you will know what each word means when you see it in your reading.

minority   (my-NAR-ih-tee) A group that is less than half of any total number; opposite of the majority.

refugee   (REH-fyoo-jee) A person who leaves his or her country for safety, often because of being punished for religious or political views.

migrate   (MY-grayt) To move from one country or area to another. A *migrant* is a person who does this.

adjust   (uh-JUST) To change so that you can fit.

heritage   (HER-ut-ij) Something that is passed on from one's ancestors; inheritance.

fast   (FAST) To stop eating for a particular period of time.

unskilled   (un-SKILD) Without training or education.

Spanish-speaking Americans

Who are *Chicanos*?
What is *La Causa*?

We have read about Blacks and their struggle for an equal place in American society. Spanish-speaking Americans are another large **minority** which has been fighting for equal treatment for many years.

Spanish-speaking Americans come from several different countries. Many Cuban **refugees** fled to America in the 1960s because they did not like the new government of Fidel Castro. They are still coming. Most of these Cubans now live in Florida.

Other Spanish-speaking Americans come here from *Puerto Rico*. They have come over the years because of the poverty and unemployment there. Puerto Rico became part of the United States after the Spanish-American War in 1898. Puerto Ricans became U.S. citizens in 1917, so it is easy for them to **migrate** here.

Most Puerto Ricans who come to America live in large cities, especially in New York, Connecticut, and New Jersey. **Adjusting** to life here is not easy for them. It is often difficult to find good-paying jobs. If they do not know English, they may need to take low-paying jobs as **unskilled** workers. This work often leaves them little time or energy for learning English, which could help them find better jobs. Many hope to return to their homeland. There is a lot of going back and forth. Because they can keep returning to Puerto Rico, they may never really feel that America is their home.

Puerto Rico is more racially integrated than America. There are so many different skin colors that it is not important whether a person is black, white, Native American, or a combination of racial backgrounds. People of different skin color live there peacefully together and often marry each other. Puerto Ricans who come to the United States find out that people here pay much more attention to differences between those who are dark skinned and those who are light. Puerto Ricans learn that it is much easier to be white than brown or black in America. ●

Most Spanish-speaking Americans do not come from Cuba or Puerto Rico, however. They come from Mexico. After Blacks, Mexican Americans are the largest racial minority in this country.

Mexican Americans today are called *Chicanos*. Most Chicanos live in California and the southwestern states, near the Mexican border, but there are some in each of our fifty states. In the past, Chicanos who moved to the United States often did not come with special job skills. They found jobs doing unskilled labor, which paid very little. Many did farm work.

6

PWER-to REE-kow

chee-KAN-os

40

Like Blacks and like other Spanish-speaking Americans, Chicanos often have a hard time living in America. They are thought of as "different" because of their darker skin color and because they speak Spanish. Most Chicanos are proud of their Mexican **heritage** and want to continue to speak their native Spanish. But they need to know English to get along in this country. American schools have not been very sympathetic to this problem. Sometimes schools teach only in English and refuse to allow children to speak Spanish. Chicanos are made to feel that their culture and their skills are worthless. They are made to feel that the white American way of life is the only way to live.

Because of the language problem, many Chicano students have a hard time in school. If they do well, it is sometimes because they have learned to act like white Americans, or "Anglos." They learn that living the way they did in their own country will not help them get ahead here. They are told they will do better if they can speak English without a Spanish accent and if they try to be part of American *culture*.

KUL-cher

Many Chicanos live in cities in crowded *barrios*, or slums. Children often have to quit school and go to work to help the family. If they do not finish their education, it is even harder for them to find good jobs when they are adults.

BAH-ree-ohss

A large number of Chicanos who live in the country work as migrant farm workers. They move from farm to farm, harvesting each new crop as it comes in season. The workers' pay is low, and working conditions are poor. They have no chance to settle down in one place. Because they move around so often, their children do not have much chance to go to school.

Chicanos are fighting for better living and working conditions. The Supreme Court decision against school segregation has helped. It made it illegal for Chicano children to be set apart in poor schools. Another law, passed in 1968, said that all teachers of Mexican Americans should know about Mexico's heritage and should be able to speak both English and Spanish. ●

One important Chicano leader is a farm worker named Cesar *Chavez*. In the 1960s Chavez organized a group of California grape pickers into the United Farm Workers' union. He demanded better conditions and better pay for the union members. Dolores *Huerta* was vice president of the Farm Workers. The grape growers did everything they could — including using violence — to fight the union.

SHAH-vez

WAIR-tuh

Like Dr. Martin Luther King, Jr., Chavez is against violence. He did not want his followers to fight with the grape growers. When some Chicanos threatened to beat up the growers, Chavez went on a **fast**. He did not eat for twenty-four days. The union members worried that he would die. They promised not to use violence, so Chavez began eating again.

Chavez's peaceful methods worked. He organized a *huelga* (strike) against the grape growers in order to get them to meet his demands. When this was not enough, he urged everyone to stop buying grapes. The boycott was a success. The grape growers sold fewer grapes and lost money. They then agreed to some of the Farm Workers' demands.

WAYL-guh

Other Chicano leaders have not been as peaceful and *patient* as Chavez. *Reies Lopez Tijerina*, the "Little Tiger," believed that Chicanos should be allowed to use land that the United States had stolen from them years ago. He was put in jail several times as a result of his protesting. Rodolfo "Corky" *Gonzales* wanted to form a new Chicano political party and, some day, a nation of Mexican Americans separate from the United States. Gonzales hoped to bring back the glory of his Aztec ancestors.

PAY-shunt
RAY-ess LOH-pez
ti-er-EE-nuh

gon-ZAH-less

Cesar Chavez has said that his work for La Causa (the cause of helping Chicanos) will take him a lifetime. He believes that even if Chicanos cannot make the world better for themselves, perhaps they can build a happier life for their children and grandchildren.

Mexican Americans, Cuban Americans, and Puerto Ricans are all Spanish-speaking Americans living in the United States. While they differ from each other in many ways, they share several goals. They want to be treated fairly and to have equal opportunities for good education and good jobs. And they want to be able to express pride in their heritage, not forced to *deny* it.

dee-NY

Answer these to review the main ideas.

A.

1. Who are the Chicanos? Where do they come from? _____

_____

_____

2. What are some of the problems that Chicanos face? _____

_____

_____

3. Who is Cesar Chavez? What does he think about violence? _____

_____

_____

How does Chavez get things done for his people? _____

_____

_____

_____

4. Who else besides Chicanos are Spanish-speaking Americans? _____

_____

Why do they come to the United States? _____

_____

Circle the right answer to finish each sentence.   B.

1. Next to Blacks, the largest racial minority in the United States is

   a. Native Americans   b. Mexican   c. Spanish-speaking
                            Americans   Americans

2. A *barrio* is

   a. a bar   b. a forest   c. a city slum

3. Migrant workers are paid

   a. high wages   b. low wages   c. no wages at all

4. The United Farm Workers is

   a. a labor union   b. an insurance   c. a bank
                            company

5. *La Causa* means

   a. because   b. the race   c. the cause of
                                                 helping Chicanos

Circle True or False.   C.

T F 1. Mexican Americans have had trouble in school because classes are often taught in English.

T F 2. Cesar Chavez said that the best way to get ahead in life is to use violence.

T F 3. Chicano migrant farmers worked for California grape growers.

T F 4. The boycott against the grape growers worked well.

T F 5. No Spanish is spoken in either Cuba or Puerto Rico.

Choose one of these words to fit each sentence below.

migrate   refugee   heritage

minority   adjust   fast

unskilled

1. Mexican Americans are a _____ in the United States today.

2. Leaders will sometimes go on a _____ when they want to correct something that is wrong.

3. It is often hard to _____ to life in a new country.

4. It is easy for Puerto Ricans to _____ to the United States.

5. Most Chicanos are proud of their Mexican _____.

6. She was a _____ from fascism.

7. _____ workers usually earn low wages.

Think about and discuss in class.

Compare the Black and Chicano movements over the last twenty years or so. Start by reading about and discussing Martin Luther King, Jr., and Cesar Chavez. How are the two men alike? How much progress have

Blacks and Chicanos made toward gaining equal rights? _____

_____

_____

_____

Would you be willing to fast, the way Cesar Chavez did? Do fasts work?

_____

_____

Have you ever seen people on strike outside a store or factory? What did

the strikers do? _____

_____

_____

How did they explain the reasons for their strike? _____

_____

D.

E.

44

Many Native Americans live on reservations. Their original way of life is nearly gone.

Getting Ready for Chapter Seven

7

Here are five vocabulary words that are used in the story of Native Americans*. Study these definitions so you will know what each word means when you see it in your reading.

native   (NAY-tiv) Born in a particular place; a native is a person who belongs to a particular country or place by right of birth.

reservation   (reh-zur-VAY-shun) Something kept or reserved for special use; a piece of land kept for use only by Native Americans.

epidemic   (eh-pih-DEH-mik) An outbreak of a disease that spreads rapidly and affects large numbers of people at the same time.

honor   (ON-ur) To treat with respect; to show high regard and appreciation for.

values   (VAL-yooz) Things you believe in and think are important.

*When Columbus came to this part of the world he thought he had reached the islands of the East *Indies* near India. So he called the people who were here Indians. This word has come to have so many bad stereotypes attached to it that most Native Americans prefer that it not be used.

IN-deez

White men made treaties with Native Americans which allowed them to take over Native American lands. The problems arising from these unfair treaties are still being discussed.

Life on reservations is managed by the U.S. Bureau of Indian Affairs. Most Native Americans feel strongly that the Bureau does not meet their needs.

Native Americans

Why don't most Native Americans like to be called Indians?
What does the Bureau of Indian Affairs do?

On Thanksgiving Day, 1977, fifty **Native** Americans began a fast at Plymouth, Massachusetts. While other Americans feasted to celebrate the holiday, these Americans ate nothing. When asked why they were fasting, they replied that they had nothing to give thanks for.

Nearly two million Native Americans live in the United States today. Some live on **reservations** in the West and Southwest. Others live in cities or towns. Many are poor, live in poor housing, and have low-paying jobs or no jobs at all. Over the years, the European immigrants and settlers have nearly destroyed the Native American way of life.

Native Americans were the first people to live in this country. They lived in the Americas long before the *European* settlers came. When Columbus arrived here there were about ten to twelve million people already living in North America. There were many different Native groups, each with its own customs and ways of life. During the next four hundred years many groups were wiped out in **epidemics** of disease which were brought from Europe by white men. Others were barely able to survive as they were forced off the lands that provided their food. By the late 1800s there were only a quarter of a million Native Americans left.

yoor-uh-PEE-un

Sometimes the settlers and the Native Americans were friends, but the two groups had very different **values**. For example, Native Americans thought land was a gift from the gods for everyone to share, while the whites believed that each person should own as much property as he or she could. Whites claimed that the lands they took or "bought" from Native populations belonged to them forever. When they decided they wanted more land, they sometimes just took it at gunpoint. Native nations fought hard and tried to remain on their land.

Often the white men did make treaties with the Native peoples. These treaties gave the Natives the right to stay on certain areas of land called reservations. When the settlers wanted these lands later on, however, they would simply break the treaties and take the land. This went on until there was almost no land left for Native Americans. ●

Today Native Americans are U.S. citizens. Thousands live in big cities like New York, *Seattle*, and Los Angeles. They live and work like everyone else. But most of them are poor. They have had poor education, and many have been the victims of prejudice.

see-AT-ul

For those who decide to stay on the reservations, life is also hard. They live in huts and cabins, some without running water or electricity.

There are usually not enough jobs to go around, and schools are often poor.

Reservations today are run by the government. The *Bureau* of Indian Affairs (BIA) is in Washington, D.C. It manages life on the reservation. It decides how the schools are run. Native American children are usually taught the values of the white culture. They are not taught their own history or values. The Bureau has not met the needs of Native Americans. Native Americans do not want to have a Bureau telling them what to do. They want to run their own lives.

BYOO-row

Native Americans are angry at all that has been taken away from them. They have been making their feelings clear.

In 1972, a group of several hundred Native Americans rode together across the United States to Washington, D.C. They called this trip the Trail of Broken Treaties. They wanted to remind Americans of all the promises to the Native nations that the government had broken. The Native American group managed to get inside the Bureau of Indian Affairs headquarters. They were protesting the treatment of Native Americans today as well as in the past.

Native Americans have gone to court to get back a lot of their land. They have won in some cases. Some of their demands for better treatment and more power to govern themselves are also being listened to. Native nations now have more power to plan and run their own programs on reservations, but they cannot make decisions without the approval of the BIA.

Native Americans feel that they should have better schools, health care, housing, and jobs. But they don't want to blend completely into American society. They want their own values and way of life to be **honored**, not destroyed. Native Americans today want America to make up for its crimes of the past by honoring old treaty rights, returning stolen land, and letting them determine their own futures.

Answer these to review the main ideas.

A.

1. What are some of the problems Native Americans face today? _____

_____

_____

2. How did white settlers and Native Americans differ in their ideas

about owning land? _____

_____

_____

3. How did the white settlers try to make Native Americans more like white people? _____

_____

4. What does the Bureau of Indian Affairs do? _____

_____

_____

5. Why are Native Americans not satisfied with the Bureau? _____

_____

6. Why do Native Americans dislike being called Indians? _____

_____

_____

B.

Circle True or False.

T   F   1. Native Americans fasted during a 1977 Thanksgiving.

T   F   2. Native Americans took away lands from the white settlers.

T   F   3. Living conditions on the first reservations for Native Americans were usually poor.

T   F   4. Native Americans wanted to learn how to be like whites.

T   F   5. The white settlers broke many treaties made with the Native nations.

T   F   6. Native nations on reservations are running their own affairs more and more.

C.

Circle the right answer to finish each sentence.

1. The Native Americans had a fast because they

   a. had nothing to   b. were running   c. were obeying a
      give thanks for   out of food   religious custom

2. Europeans settled in America

   a. long before the   b. many years   c. at the same time
      Native   after the Native   as the Native
      Americans   Americans   Americans

3. White settlers took away Native American lands and

    a. customs   b. arrows   c. reservations

4. Native Americans today can live

    a. only on   b. only in   c. wherever they
        reservations   cities   wish

5. In Washington, a group of Native Americans captured

    a. the Capitol   b. the Senate   c. the Bureau of
                        Office Building   Indian Affairs

6. Native Americans feel it is important that they

    a. be like white   b. keep their   c. live only on
        society   tribal heritage   reservations

D. Choose one of these words to fit each sentence below.

values   honor   epidemic

reservation   native

1. She is a _____ of France, but she spent most of her life in Italy.

2. Living on a _____ makes many Native Americans unhappy.

3. An _____ of the flu caused many students to stay home from school.

4. She was very upset that he did not _____ his agreement with her.

5. Their _____ are different from ours. They believe every person should look out for himself; we believe people should look out for each other.

E. Think about and discuss in class.

Find out what happened when some Native Americans took over Wounded Knee, South Dakota, in 1973. Look up other Native American protests which have taken place in the last few years (e.g., those of the Cree people in Quebec whose land will be flooded if plans for a hydroelectric power plant are carried out).

White Americans sometimes say that it was not wrong for white settlers to take land from the Native Americans. They say that the Native nations "did nothing" with the land, but the white settlers took over and built America into a great nation. What do you think of this argument?

_____

_____

_____

_____

Women met at Seneca Falls, New York, in 1848 and wrote a statement demanding complete political, social, religious, and economic equality.

WOMAN'S CAUSE IS MAN'S THEY RISE OR FALL TOGETHER

Women fought for the right to vote for seventy-two years. They finally won in 1920.

In the 1800s women began to work in mills. They were paid less than half of what men were paid.

Getting Ready for Chapter Eight

Here are seven vocabulary words that are used in the story about equal rights for women. Study these definitions so you will know what each word means when you see it in your reading.

depend   (dee-PEND) Lean on another person; count on someone else for help.

suffrage   (SUF-rij) The right to vote.

coeducation   (koh-eh-joo-KAY-shun) Having both men and women at the same school.

pregnant   (PREG-nunt) Having a baby growing inside the body.

ratify   (RAT-ih-fy) Approve.

feminist   (FEM-ih-nist) A person who supports the movement for the equality of men and women in politics, society, and the economy.

economic   (ee-kuh-NOM-ik) Having to do with money or business.

Women's Fight for Equal Rights

What was the Seneca Falls Convention?
What is the Equal Rights Amendment?

How many women doctors do you know of? How many women governors, senators, or company presidents? Has the president of the United States ever been a woman? Even though more than half of American women now work outside the home, most of their jobs are at lower levels and pay less than men's jobs do.

We have been reading about groups of people who do not have equal rights in our country — American Blacks, Native Americans, and Chicanos. Now we will study still another large group fighting for equal treatment — women.

In the past, women were taught that their place was at home. A woman's job was to marry, to serve her husband, and to be a good mother and housekeeper while the man of the family went out to earn a living. Men were the rulers of the family. They told women and children what to do. In colonial days, women could not own any property or sign *business* papers. Until long after the Civil War most women were not able to get much education. Married women were forced to **depend** on men completely. They could not have their own money. They could not serve on juries or make a will. They were the property of their husbands. In some ways their lives were like Blacks'. ●

BIZ-ness

In the 1800s the lives of everyone changed a lot. Machines began to do many of the jobs once done by hand. The spinning and weaving work that had been done at home now was completed in a factory or mill. Many families were very poor, so widows, unmarried women, and children went to work in mills and factories. They worked long hours — sometimes more than fourteen hours a day. They were paid less than half of what men were paid.

Large numbers of women workers organized and began to strike. Their strikes were not very successful. They didn't have enough time to organize since they also had work to do at home after a long day of work in the factory. In addition, because many immigrants were arriving in America, looking for work, factory owners could hire them to take the jobs of workers who were on strike. Immigrants needed work so much that they would take very low wages and endure bad working conditions and not complain.

In 1848 women held a convention at Seneca Falls, New York. Over 100 men and women wrote a statement that was like the Declaration of Independence. It demanded complete political, social, religious, and **economic** equality for women. This convention was the beginning of the women's **suffrage** movement. For seventy-two years women fought for the right to vote. They finally won in 1920. Congress passed the Nineteenth Amendment to the Constitution, which says that the right of citizens to vote cannot be taken away because of their sex.

In the early 1800s most high schools did not admit women. In 1833, Oberlin became the first **coeducational** college, but it would not let women take the same courses as men until eleven years later. By the late 1800s middle- and upper-class white women were winning their fight for high school and college education, but most poor women and Black women still had very little chance even to learn to read and write. ●

One of the most important things women have fought for over the years is the right to plan the size of their own families. By the early 1900s some women knew how to keep from getting **pregnant.** Poor women, though, suffered a lot because of pregnancies which they could not afford. Many died trying to end these pregnancies. Still more babies and mothers died because of the poverty they lived in. A nurse named Margaret Sanger fought for the right of women to get information about birth control. She won her fight in 1937, when the U.S. Court of Appeals said that doctors had the right to give *patients* this information.

PAY-shunts

In 1973, the U.S. Supreme Court ruled on a woman's right to choose whether or not to end a pregnancy (to have an abortion). In the case of *Roe v. Wade*, the Court said that no state could prevent a woman's choice to have an abortion during the first six months of pregnancy. They said this decision was part of an individual's constitutional right to privacy. In the years following the ruling, there have been many arguments between groups who support it and those who do not. Even though a majority of Americans say they support a woman's right to decide, groups who oppose abortion have used civil disobedience and court cases to change the law. Often, these groups also oppose providing any information about birth control.

In the 1960s the Women's Liberation Movement became a strong force for equal pay, equal rights, and an equal partnership in the home. **Feminists** have also been struggling for an end to sex stereotyping — to thinking that some things are things that only girls do and some things are things that only boys do. They also believe that women have a right to be respected and independent — whether they are married or unmarried.

In 1972, Congress passed the Equal Rights Amendment to the Constitution (ERA). The ERA said that equality of rights under the law could not be taken away on account of sex. In order to become a law this amendment had to be ratified by two-thirds of the states. In

1982, the deadline for passage of the ERA, only thirty of the thirty-three states required had approved it, and so the Equal Rights Amendment did not become law. But even if it had passed, the ERA would not have improved the daily lives of most women. Black, Puerto Rican, and Chicano women continue to have lower-level and lower-paying jobs than white women. And in order for women to have real equality, both men and women need day-care arrangements and work *schedules* which allow them to be parents as well as workers.

SKED-jools

Nevertheless, progress has been made. Some women are now doctors, lawyers, soldiers, sailors, and scientists. Many men and women share child-care and other household tasks; many women have full, independent lives without being married or having children. The women's movement keeps working to change the way people think about men and women, and to make sure that *all* women share in the progress toward full equality.

Answer these to review the main ideas.

A.

1. What are some of the rights which have been denied to women over the years? _____

_____

_____

2. What was one of the first big victories in women's fight for equal rights? _____

_____

_____

3. What are some demands of the modern women's movement? What changes, other than legal ones, do women want to see? _____

_____

_____

_____

4. What was the Equal Rights Amendment? _____

_____

5. What did the Supreme Court rule in the case of *Roe v. Wade*? _____

_____

_____

Circle True or False.

T F 1. Women went to work in factories in the 1800s because of the good pay.

T F 2. Men have always wanted women to get out of the kitchen and find office jobs.

T F 3. The Seneca Falls Convention was the beginning of the women's suffrage movement.

T F 4. More than half of all American women today hold jobs outside the home.

T F 5. Many feminists think men should be able to stay home and take care of their children if they choose to.

Circle the right answer to finish each sentence.

1. Most women in America could get little education until

   a. after the American Revolution
   b. after the Civil War
   c. after the Nineteenth Amendment was passed

2. Women won the right to vote in

   a. 1776
   b. 1860
   c. 1920

3. In colonial days, women

   a. were the heads of their families
   b. shared responsibility with their husbands
   c. had no power at all

4. Margaret Sanger fought for women's right to

   a. vote
   b. control the size of their families
   c. strike

5. The Equal Rights Amendment said that women could

   a. not work wherever they wished
   b. not be in the army
   c. not be discriminated against on account of sex

Choose one of these words to fit each sentence below.

depend   coeducation   ratified

suffrage   pregnant   feminist

economic

1. Even though she was _____ she played tennis until just before the baby was born.

2. Because women had no money or power of their own they had to _____ on men.

3. The campaign for women's _____ began at Seneca Falls.

4. The Equal Rights Amendment did not become law because not enough states _____ it.

5. My mother has always been a strong _____.

6. Women wanted political, religious, and _____ equality.

7. Early educators were not in favor of _____.

Think about and discuss in class.

Do you think women should have full equal rights with men? Explain the reasons for your view. _____

_____

_____

_____

Do you think it is important to change words in the English language (such as chairman, businessman, fireman) so that they refer to women as well as to men? Why or why not? _____

_____

_____

Why do you think women have been discriminated against for so long?

_____

_____

Getting Ready for Chapter Nine

9

Here are seven vocabulary words which are used in the story about the space age. Study these definitions so you will know what each word means when you see it in your reading.

rocket   (RAH-ket) A jet engine that carries its own oxygen for burning fuel.

satellite   (SAT-ih-lite) A body that circles around a larger body in space. The earth is a satellite of the sun. Also, countries that are controlled by stronger countries.

research   (REE-surch) Careful looking up and studying in order to find new information.

achievement   (uh-CHEEV-munt) Something done by great effort.

astronaut   (AS-truh-not) A traveler in a spaceship.

gravity   (GRAV-ih-tee) The pull of the earth on all the objects near its surface.

planet   (PLAN-ut) One of the bodies that revolves around the sun.

In 1957 we enlarged our space program so we could compete with the Soviet Union. Both countries thought that rockets and satellites could be important weapons.

Astronaut John Glenn's spacecraft circled the earth three times and then parachuted into the ocean.

Two American astronauts landed on the moon in the *Apollo 11* spaceship in 1969.

The Space Age

Why was there a "space race"?
What are some of America's successes and failures in space?

During the years of the Cold War the Soviet Union and the United States were having a "space race." **Research** in outer space was important to both countries. They felt that if they ever went to war, **rockets** and **satellites** would be useful and important weapons.

In 1957 the Soviets took a big step forward. They launched a powerful rocket which carried a satellite — a metal ball about the size of a basketball. The satellite went around the earth every ninety minutes or so and sent back messages from space. Sometimes it was as far as 500 miles away.

The Soviets were proud of their **achievement**, but the American government was worried. We were afraid that this gave the Soviet Union an edge over us, so we decided to spend more time and money on space research.

In 1957 we enlarged our space program. Americans wanted schools to teach more math and science. Then someday there would be more *engineers* who could build bigger and better rockets and satellites. Congress approved billions of dollars to spend on education and space programs. America tried to launch its first satellite late in 1957, but the rocket burned up before it could get off the ground.

One month after their first satellite went up, the Soviets launched another one. This was larger than the first. It carried a trained dog named *Laika* (which means "Little Barker"). The Soviets wanted to find out how space travel would affect a living thing. The satellite circled the earth for seven days.

The Soviets were doing more and more. In 1961, they sent the first person into space. *Yuri Gagarin* went around the globe in a rocket in less than two hours. At times he went as fast as 18,000 miles an hour. Compare this to the 55-mile-per-hour speed limit of cars today! ●

When President Kennedy took office in 1961, he decided to speed up our space program. He said that the United States would work to have a man on the moon before 1970.

In May 1961, Alan B. Shepard, Jr., became the first American to travel in space. Shepard flew 300 miles in fifteen minutes. It was a short trip, but it was a beginning. The U.S. moved on to longer space trips in 1962, when **astronaut** John Glenn circled the earth three times and returned safely. Glenn's spacecraft *parachuted* into the ocean. Ships were waiting nearby, and American sailors picked him up and carried him to land.

9

en-jin-EERZ

LY-kuh

YOO-ree
gah-GAH-reen

PA-ruh-shoo-ted

In 1969 the great dream came true: Americans landed on the moon. We wanted to go to the moon because it is much closer to us than the stars are. It would take thousands of years of travel to reach many stars, but the moon is only a three - or four-day rocket flight from earth.

Neil Armstrong commanded the *Apollo 11* space ship on the first trip to the moon. With him were astronauts Edwin Aldrin and Michael Collins. The spacecraft blasted off from Cape Kennedy in Florida on July 16, 1969.

The *Apollo 11* space capsule had enough *fuel* to get to the moon and back, enough food and water, and a special machine to make oxygen for breathing. The three men were weightless because there is no **gravity** in space. Things and people will float if they are not tied down.

FYOO-ul

When the Apollo crew reached the moon, they went around it several times. They saw no signs of life. The moon looked like an empty *desert*, filled with dust, sand, craters, and big rocks.

DEH-zert

Armstrong looked for a safe place to land on the moon. He did not want to hit a rock or to land on the edge of a crater. If the space ship were hurt in any way, it might not be able to return to earth. The astronauts would die without food, air, or water.

The space ship made a safe landing. Armstrong slowly climbed down onto the moon's surface, followed by Aldrin. They wore special space suits which allowed them to breathe and protected them from small flying rocks or sand. Back on earth, the largest number of people in the history of television were watching a live broadcast of the moonwalk.

After planting an American flag in the sand, Armstrong and Aldrin went exploring. Because there is very little gravity on the moon to hold them down, they hopped from place to place like kangaroos. They collected rocks and soil to bring back to earth for scientists to study. They also set up a machine to measure earthquakes (or moonquakes) and send the measurements to earth.

The trip to the moon was successful. When the astronauts returned to earth President Nixon greeted them. Then they were examined by doctors. They had to be kept by themselves for three weeks to make sure that they hadn't brought back any new *germs* from the moon. ●

JURMZ

America had won the race to the moon. The Soviets continued with their own plans. They sent unmanned space ships to the moon to take pictures and collect soil and rock samples.

Since the American flight to the moon, NASA (National *Aeronautics* and Space Administration) has had many plans for further space pro-

ayr-uh-NAW-tix

rams. One of these is called the space shuttle. Spacecraft carrying astronauts are launched by rockets into the sky. On board are satellites, carrying large cameras and telescopes. Out in space, the astronauts release the satellites, which swing around the earth by themselves, held in place by the force of gravity. The cameras send back pictures of the weather on earth, so that we can be warned of storms or floods. The giant telescopes on board the satellites use mirrors to magnify distant objects. Satellites also make telephone and television communications between continents possible.

But, in 1986, tragedy struck the space program. The space shuttle *Challenger* was launched from Cape Canaveral, Florida. On board were scientists and a schoolteacher named Christa McAuliffe. The teacher was to give lessons from space to students who were watching on television. What the students saw was shocking beyond belief. The *Challenger* caught fire ten miles above earth and fell in flaming pieces into the sea. All aboard were killed in a matter of seconds.

Because of this terrible event, the space program was forced to proceed much more slowly and cautiously. Even so, it has continued to have problems. In 1990, the Hubble telescope, which had a huge mirror, was launched in space. There were hopes that the mirror on this telescope would be able to pick out stars never seen before. But when scientists started receiving the first photographs, they learned that the mirror had a defect. It had never been tested while it was on earth. They are now planning to repair it in space.

NASA has launched unmanned spaceships that travel millions of miles away from earth. With no one aboard, they automatically send back information about Mars, Venus, and other **planets** which astronauts may visit in person some day.

Finally, NASA has also made plans for a huge space station that would remain in the atmosphere permanently. It would carry six to eight astronauts. But the space station will cost billions of dollars. When there are many other parts of American life that need money so much, it is not certain that the government will budget it for space.

Answer these to review the main ideas.

A.

1. Why were Soviets and Americans doing space research? _____

_____

2. Why did Americans worry when the Soviets were ahead in the space

race? _____

_____

3. What did America do to enlarge its space program? _____

_____

4. Who was Yuri Gagarin? _____

_____

5. How does the space shuttle program work? _____

_____

_____

6. What is one reason people might not be in favor of exploring space?

_____

_____

B. Circle True or False.

T   F   1. In 1957 the Soviets sent a man into space.

T   F   2. Americans wanted students to learn more history so they could help someday in the space program.

T   F   3. President Kennedy wanted to spend money on the space program.

T   F   4. The moon is closer to earth than the stars we see at night.

T   F   5. Satellites help us predict weather.

C. Circle the right answer to finish each sentence.

1. The first Soviet satellite circled the earth

   a. every 90 minutes   b. once a week   c. once a year

2. The first satellite rocket Americans launched

   a. worked well   b. burned up   c. was better than the Russians'

3. People in space

   a. are so heavy   b. can't see   c. float because
      they can't move   they have no
                                                   weight

Choose one of these words to fit each sentence below.

rocket   research   gravity   planet

satellite   achievement   astronaut

. We are pulled to the surface of the earth by _____.

. Neil Armstrong was the first _____ to set foot on the moon.

. Her _____ helped her to come up with a new idea about how the space shuttle might work.

. That _____ is carrying both a camera and a telescope.

. Mars, Jupiter, and other _____s revolve around the sun.

. The scientists were very proud of their _____s.

. The scientists were trying to find a new kind of fuel for the

_____.

Think about and discuss in class.

Have you heard anything in the news lately about exploring space? Are there plans for future space investigations? _____

_____

_____

Do you think it is important to spend money on space exploration? Why or why not? _____

_____

_____

Do you think that space should belong to the country that explores it first? Do you think it should belong to everyone? Why? _____

_____

_____

D.

E.

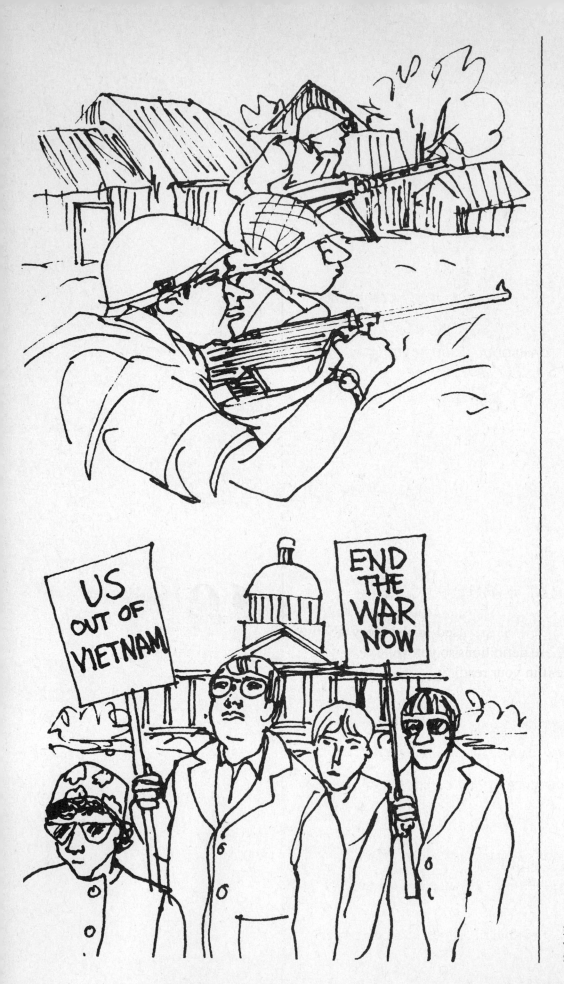

American soldiers fought in jungles and villages. They destroyed large pa[rt] of Vietnam trying to keep it from becoming a communist country.

Millions of Americans protested the war. They demanded an end to the fighting.

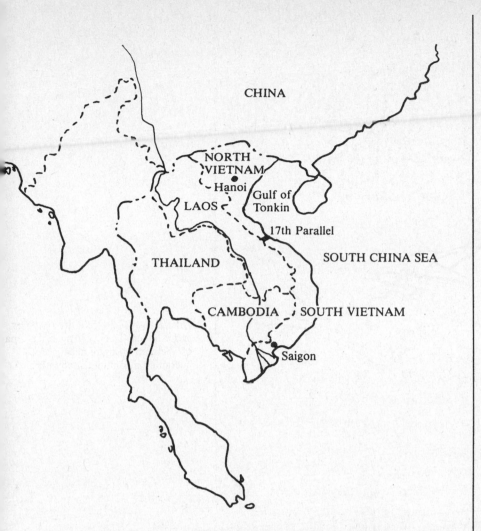

Getting Ready for Chapter Ten

10

Here are seven vocabulary words that are used in the story about America's longest war. Study these definitions so you will know what each word means when you see it in your reading.

colony   (KOL-uh-nee) A country, usually far away, which is ruled by another country.

international (in-tur-NASH-un-ul) Among many countries.

guerrilla   (guh-RIL-luh) A person who is part of a group of people who are not in a regular army but who are fighting in a war — often against the government.

trudging   (TRUJ-ing) To walk on and on, usually in a tired way.

civilians   (sih-VILH-yuns) People who are not in the armed forces.

honorable   (ON-ur-uh-bul) Something or someone worth respect; noble.

massive   (MASS-iv) Huge, giant.

America's Longest War

Why was Vietnam so important to the United States?
How did the American people help to end the war?

Chapter
10

ho-chee-MIN

Vietnam, a small country in Southeast Asia, was once a French **colony**. After World War II, the Vietnamese people revolted against French rule. They wanted to run their own country — to be independent. Led by a communist named *Ho Chi Minh*, the Vietnamese fought hard for seven years and defeated the French.

An **international** conference was held in Geneva, Switzerland, in 1954. The countries at the conference agreed to a truce in Vietnam for 300 days. During this time, the French would run the area in the south. After the truce, free elections would be held throughout Vietnam. Then Vietnam would become one independent country with one government of its own choice.

The United States did not like this agreement and would not sign it. We knew Ho Chi Minh would win the election. We were against a united Vietnam led by Ho Chi Minh because it would be a communist country.

The North Vietnamese government wanted all of Vietnam to have a communist government. Many people in the South wanted this, too. But the United States wanted South Vietnam to be a separate, democratic state. We sent them $270 million per year to help keep the government we liked in power. The people in South Vietnam who wanted elections and a united country began fighting against the government in the South. They were **guerrillas** and were known as the Viet Cong. North Vietnam soon supported them in their fight, and war spread. ●

The U.S. government began to send military advisers, then more and more weapons. Slowly, America got more involved in the war. We sent more and more soldiers and weapons and began bombing the North. In 1965, President Johnson sent hundreds of thousands of troops to fight the Viet Cong and their supporters.

Fighting in Vietnam was very hard for American troops. Some South Vietnamese were friendly to the United States. Others supported the communists. It was hard to tell exactly who was the enemy.

Years went by, and neither side seemed to be winning. Many American soldiers became worried and angry. They saw that many of the South Vietnamese people did not even want Americans there. Americans were tired of **trudging** through jungles and villages. They had to be alert for sniper bullets and buried land mines and, sometimes, for attacks by people they thought were **civilians.**

68

The Viet Cong traveled in small groups, hiding in the jungle and making sudden, surprise attacks on the American forces. It was almost impossible to fight this hidden enemy. In some cases American soldiers destroyed whole villages, including women and children, just to make sure they killed any enemy soldiers who might be there.

Americans fighting on the ground destroyed large parts of South Vietnam. From the air, American bombers blew up towns and cities; they sprayed deadly pesticides, like Agent Orange, on forests and farms to kill all the plants. Large parts of North and South Vietnam lay in ruins by the end of the war.

More troops were sent to Vietnam. Stories of the horrors going on there reached American citizens. More and more people cried out against the war. They were shocked at what was happening. They protested that the South Vietnamese government run by President *Thieu* was corrupt. American and Vietnamese lives were being destroyed for no good reason. ●

TYOO

Millions of people in the U.S. took part in parades and protests, demanding an end to the fighting. College students were especially angry. In one antiwar demonstration at Kent State University in Ohio, the National Guard killed four students and wounded nine others. The Vietnam War seemed to be destroying American society as well as Vietnamese.

President Johnson had been well liked by the American people. But now the Americans blamed Johnson for the war. In the election of 1968, Johnson did not even try to run for reelection. He knew he had no chance of winning.

When Richard Nixon became president in 1968, he promised he would end the war soon. He began pulling out troops slowly, but the war became larger and *bloodier*. Nixon said he wanted to have "peace with honor." He did not want to take away all American support from the South Vietnamese government. He said he did not want to leave captured American prisoners behind.

BLUH-dee-er

Peace talks with the communists were started in Paris in 1972. Nixon continued slowly taking out troops, but he also kept bombing North Vietnam even while he was winding down the war.

At last in 1973 the end came. America agreed to pull out all forces if the communists would release the American prisoners of war held in Vietnam. South Vietnam was left to rule itself. In 1975, North Vietnamese troops and the Viet Cong captured *Saigon*, the capital of South Vietnam. The communists took over the government of the south.

sy-GON

After thirteen years the war was over for Americans. The POWs went home safely. But many Americans did not see anything **honorable** about the loss of 58,000 American lives and billions of dollars.

We were not proud of the **massive** destruction which took place in that small country.

The Vietnam War was a lesson to America. Congress passed an act that says a president cannot send American forces to war without the permission of Congress. Just about everyone agrees that in the future we must be more careful about the wars we get into.

Answer these to review the main ideas.

A.

1. Why did the United States go to war in Vietnam? _____

_____

_____

2. Why was it especially difficult for American soldiers to fight in

   Vietnam? _____

_____

3. How did the people of South Vietnam feel about the war? _____

_____

_____

4. Why did so many American citizens protest the war? How did they

   show their anger? What happened at Kent State University? _____

_____

_____

_____

5. Why didn't President Nixon end the war right away? _____

_____

_____

6. How did the Vietnam War finally end? _____

_____

_____

Circle True or False.

T F 1. Ho Chi Minh was a communist leader.

T F 2. American soldiers fighting in Vietnam found it hard to tell their friends from their enemies.

T F 3. Most American college students were in favor of the war in Vietnam.

T F 4. The Viet Cong helped America fight in Vietnam.

T F 5. The Vietnam War made President Johnson very popular.

T F 6. After the United States left Vietnam, the communists took over the government of the South.

B.

Circle the right answer to finish each sentence.

1. Vietnam once belonged to

   a. France   b. Spain   c. Portugal

2. According to the Geneva Conference in 1954, Vietnam should be

   a. divided into   b. a united country   c. run by France
      two countries

3. The capital of South Vietnam was

   a. Saigon   b. My Lai   c. Pleiku

4. The president who sent large numbers of troops to Vietnam in 1965 was

   a. Johnson   b. Nixon   c. Kennedy

C.

Choose one of these words to fit each sentence below.

massive   honorable   colony

trudging   civilians   guerrilla

international

1. There was a _____ public meeting to protest the war.

2. We wanted to end the war in an _____ way.

3. The soldiers were _____ through the jungle.

4. They were shooting at _____, although they were not supposed to.

D.

71

5. The _____s in the jungle were very hard to find.

6. It was an _____ meeting, with people from all over the world there.

7. Vietnam had been a _____ of France.

Think about and discuss in class.

Do you think it is right for soldiers to kill women and children if they think the women and children might try to kill them? _____

_____

_____

_____

Would you have gone to help America fight in Vietnam, even if you thought the war was wrong? If so, why? If not, what would you have done? _____

_____

_____

_____

Did anyone win the war in Vietnam? Explain your answer. _____

_____

_____

_____

Special Senate committees were set up to investigate both the Watergate break-in and the Iran-Contra affair. The hearings were televised.

Getting Ready for Chapter Eleven

11

Here are eight vocabulary words that are used in the story about trouble in Washington. Study these definitions so you will know what each word means when you see it in your reading.

investigation   (in-ves-tih-GAY-shun) Looking into and studying something carefully in order to find out about it.

aide   (AYD) An assistant or helper.

suspicious   (sus-PISH-hus) Having a feeling that something might be wrong.

bribe   (BRYB) A favor or a gift given to someone to persuade him or her to do something, which is usually dishonest.

perjury   (PUR-jur-ee) Telling a lie when you have sworn under oath (promised) to tell the truth.

gung-ho   (gung-HO) Too enthusiastic; extremely eager.

illegal   (ih-LEE-gul) Against the law.

patriotic   (PAY-tree-OT-ic) Loving one's country.

Secret agents working for the Republican Party broke into the headquarters of the Democratic Committee in the Watergate building in Washington. They stole papers containing campaign plans.

President Nixon resigned rather than face a trial of impeachment. He was the first president to do so.

Trouble in Washington

How did the Watergate burglary lead to a president resigning?
What happened in the Iran-Contra Affair?

Suppose you were president of the United States — What would you do first? Would you make any changes? What kind?

The president of the United States is the leader of our country. But he or she is also just the opposite. The president is the *servant* of the American people. He or she must listen to what they say. The president can be forced or voted out of office for doing a poor job.

SIR-vent

President Richard Nixon ran into this kind of trouble in 1972. Nixon was a Republican, running for reelection that year. The Republicans wanted to beat the Democrats and put Nixon back in the White House.

One of Nixon's supporters had an idea. He said the Republicans should learn what the Democrats' *campaign* plans were. Then they could trick the Democrats and win the election.

kam-PAYN

The Republicans sent spies to Democratic headquarters at the Watergate building in Washington. In the dark of night the spies, carrying flashlights and burglary tools, broke into the building. Just as they were stealing the plans, they were caught and arrested. The burglars were sent to jail.

Investigations by the courts and the United States Senate followed. They learned that some of the burglars were **aides** of President Nixon. People began to question: How much did the president himself know about the crime? Was he guilty, too? President Nixon said he knew nothing, but many people were **suspicious**.

Then the Senate investigating committee learned that Nixon had made secret tape recordings of his phone calls and conversations at work. The committee asked him to release the tapes so they could learn more about Watergate. Nixon refused. He said the tapes contained secret messages that enemies of the United States would like to have.

The president was now in deep trouble. To make matters worse, at the same time, his vice president, Spiro Agnew, had to resign from office. Agnew was charged with taking **bribes** from business people. Other Nixon assistants were sent to jail for **perjury**.

Finally, the Supreme Court ruled that Nixon had to release the tapes. The people, they argued, had the right to know the truth. Nixon knew that the courts are the law of the land and that he must obey the law, just as every other citizen must. After a time, he turned over copies of several of the tapes, as ordered.

The tapes showed that Nixon *had* known about the Watergate burglary right after it happened. He had tried to protect those who took part. He had tried to keep the country from finding out about it. The president had broken the law.

In 1974 the House of Representatives voted to impeach President Nixon for his part in the Watergate cover-up. Nixon thus became the first president since President Andrew Johnson to face removal from office. Rather than go to trial, Nixon resigned, the first president of the United States to do so. Nevertheless, a month later, he was pardoned for any crimes he "committed or may have committed." The pardon was given by the next president, Gerald Ford, who had been Nixon's vice president. ●

The president in the executive branch and the Congress in the legislative branch need to work together to make the laws of this country (see book 2, chapter 2). If they can't reach any agreement, problems can develop.

In the 1980s the president and Congress disagreed about how to act toward *Nicaragua*, a small country in Central America. In the late 1970s the people of Nicaragua had overthrown the dictator, *Anastasio Somoza*, who had run the country for over thirty years. The new government leaders, known as *Sandinistas*, worked to rebuild their country and to make a better life for the Nicaraguan people. Several countries offered them money and other aid. Among these were the Soviet Union and Cuba.

NIK-a-RA-gua
ah-nah-STA-si-o
sa-MOS-ah
SAN-di-NEES-tahs

President Ronald Reagan did not like the Sandinistas because they accepted help from communist nations. Instead, Reagan supported a small anti-communist group of Nicaraguans called *Contras*, who opposed the Sandinistas. Many of the Contras had served under the dictator, Somoza. Even so, President Reagan asked Congress to vote money for the Contras.

KON-truz

Congress was divided on the question. Some members disliked the Sandinistas, but thought even less of the Contras, whose leaders were often dishonest. Others argued that the United States had no business interfering with Nicaragua at all. Congress passed a law forbidding any government money or other help for the Contras.

At this point President Reagan's aides on the National Security Council went into action. The National Security Council advises the president on how to deal with other countries. One member of this council was a **gung-ho** Marine officer named Oliver North. Lieutenant Colonel North and others came up with a secret plan to help the Contras.

The Middle Eastern country of Iran (see map, page 82) wanted to buy weapons from the United States to fight its neighbor, Iraq. Such a

le was **illegal**. In addition, the United States was not friendly with
an because Iranians were involved with the kidnapping of several
eople, including Americans, in the Middle East. The victims, called
ostages, were to be held as prisoners until the kidnappers' demands
ere met. The Iranians offered to have the hostages freed if the United
tates would sell them weapons.

Hoping to rescue the prisoners, "Ollie" North secretly helped to ar-
ange arms sales to Iran. The president's men charged very high prices
nd turned some of their profits over to the Contras. But before much
wapping could be done, the deal had to be called off. A foreign
ewspaper found out what was happening. It published the story of the
rms-for-hostages exchange.

When this secret became known, it turned the United States upside
own. The president's aides had dared again to break the law! They
ad done exactly what Congress had made illegal. Everywhere people
sked, "How much does President Reagan know? Did he order North
nd the others to break the law? Is the president guilty of a crime?"

Just like President Nixon during Watergate, Mr. Reagan said he
new nothing about what had happened. Again, the Senate held many
veeks of televised hearings to find the truth of what happened. No one
roved that Mr. Reagan was guilty of a crime, and he finished out his
econd term.

Oliver North continued to claim that in helping the Contras he was
erving the best interests of the country. After a long trial, he was
iven a mild sentence which was later overturned.

It is a fine thing to be **patriotic**. Still, we have to wonder if the
Jnited States should let its citizens break the law whenever they feel it
s the right thing to do — or to break the law for any reason at all.

Answer these to review the main ideas.

. Why did secret agents raid the Democratic Party's offices in

Washington? What happened to them? _____

_____

_____

. Why did the Senate committee ask President Nixon to give them his

tape recordings? _____

_____

_____

A.

3. Why did President Nixon resign from office? _____

_____

_____

4. Who are the Sandinistas? Who were the Contras? _____

_____

_____

5. What did Oliver North do? _____

_____

_____

B.

Circle the right answer to finish each sentence.

1. Watergate was

   a. the headquarters of the Democratic Party

   b. a canal running across Washington

   c. the name of a well-known Democrat

2. President Nixon said at first that he

   a. knew all about the burglary

   b. knew nothing about it

   c. neither

3. Mr. Nixon was the first American president to

   a. go to jail

   b. resign from office

   c. be impeached

4. In Nicaragua, President Reagan wanted to help

   a. the Sandinistas

   b. the Communists

   c. the Contras

5. Oliver North was

   a. on the National Security Council

   b. a Watergate spy

   c. a Navy admiral

6. The president's men sold weapons to

   a. Cuba

   b. Iran

   c. Iraq

ircle True or False.

F 1. President Nixon said he would be happy to turn his secret tape recordings over to the Senate committee.

F 2. The secret tape recordings showed that Nixon knew about the Watergate break-in shortly after it happened.

F 3. President Nixon was reelected in 1976.

F 4. Nicaragua is a country located in Central America.

F 5. The Sandinistas and Contras fought each other in a civil war.

F 6. Oliver North sold weapons to Iran at a very high price.

hoose one of these words to fit each sentence below.

gung-ho   suspicious   aide   perjury

investigation   bribe   illegal   patriotic

. The _____ took a lot of time because many people had to be questioned.

. If you do something _____, you are breaking the law.

. They offered her a _____ to commit the crime.

. As she saluted the flag, she said, "I feel very _____ toward my country."

. The campers were _____ when they learned they could hike and swim all week and sleep in tents.

. Because he lied under oath, he was charged with _____.

. There were so many facts that pointed to him that people became _____.

. The _____ to the president helped solve the problem.

C.

D.

79

Think about and discuss in class.

Do you think the president of the United States should obey the law the way everyone else does? Or should he or she be able to choose which laws to obey? Explain your answer. _____

_____

_____

_____

Why is it bad for a country to have dishonest leaders? _____

_____

_____

_____

Why do the president and Congress sometimes disagree about passing laws? What happens? _____

_____

_____

_____

The word gung-ho was first used to describe daring U.S. Marine raiders in the South Pacific in World War II. Gung-ho people are enthusiastic and so eager to get things done that they do not always act wisely. Are there any gung-ho people in your class? Who? _____

_____

_____

_____

There have been other times in our history when people in high places in government got into trouble. Find out what happened when Presidents Grant and Harding were in office. _____

_____

_____

_____

America's top military leader in the Persian Gulf War was General Colin Powell, chairman of the Joint Chiefs of Staff.

12

Getting Ready for Chapter Twelve

Here are six vocabulary words that are used in the story of the end of the Cold War. Study these definitions so you will know what each word means when you see it in your reading.

strut
: (STRUTT) To walk proudly, as if showing off. To swagger.

reckless
: (REK-lus) Not cautious; acting without thinking about what will happen.

scowling
: (SKOW-ling) Looking angry and threatening.

bankrupt
: (BANK-rupt) Unable to pay one's debts or what one owes.

sanctions
: (SANK-shuns) Actions taken (short of war) by a group of nations to make another nation meet its demands. Blockades and boycotts are sanctions.

budget
: (BUD-jet) A list of what is earned and what is spent. A plan for using money.

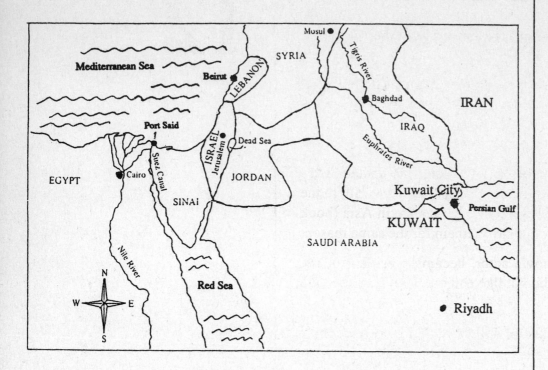

Forces of the United Nations, mostly
American, drove Iraq out of Kuwait i
the Persian Gulf war.

The End of the Cold War

What part did the United States play in the Persian Gulf War? What happened in that war?
How did the end of the Cold War change America and the world?

We Americans say that we love peace. Our presidents do not **strut** about in uniforms decorated with ribbons and medals the way leaders of some countries do. The Constitution says that our civilian presidents tell our generals what to do, not the other way around.

Because of the Cold War with the Soviet Union,* the United States used military force in a number of places throughout the world. In the Korean War we tried to stop the spread of communism in Asia (book 4). Ten years later in 1963, we fought in Vietnam for the same reason.

Ronald Reagan, a former movie actor, became president of the United States in 1980. Reagan did not like communism. He called the Soviet Union an "evil empire."

President Reagan spent billions of dollars building up America's military strength. He wanted no more defeats like Vietnam. The Soviets tried to match him by building more weapons and increasing their armed forces. Both countries went deeply into debt.

In 1985 the Soviet Union had a new leader, *Mikhail Gorbachev*. Unlike the **scowling**, unfriendly chiefs who had gone before him, Gorbachev was pleasant and often smiling. He wanted to end the Cold War with the United States. To do this, he suggested that both countries cut military spending.

The reason for this new friendliness was plain to see. The Soviet Union was going **bankrupt**. Communism wasn't working well. Farms and factories were badly managed. Stores had nothing much to sell, and people were hungry.

In 1989 the "evil empire" began to fall apart. Poland, East Germany, Hungary, and other Soviet satellites declared independence. Many people in the Soviet Union itself were sick of communism and wanted freedom and democracy.

For all his friendly ways, Gorbachev was still a communist. The restless people found a new champion in *Boris Yeltsin*, who was more democratic than Gorbachev. The two men became rivals for power. ●

The United States welcomed these changes taking place in the Soviet Union and its satellites. The danger of nuclear war with our rivals

ME-kha-el GOR-buh-chef

BOR-iss YELT-sin

---

*The Soviet Union broke up in 1991. It was replaced by a loose federation of free republics called the Commonwealth of Independent States. Russia remains the largest and most powerful republic.

was fading. We were now the strongest military power on earth. Could anyone dare to challenge us? The answer was yes — the dictator of Iraq, *Saddam Hussein*.

sa-DAM who-SANE

Iraq is a Middle Eastern country that lies between *Saudi Arabia* and Iran (see map, page 82). Many Middle Eastern countries are rich because their lands have much of the world's oil, which they sell abroad. Iraq, however, was poor and bankrupt after a long war with Iran. The Iraqis depended on selling their oil to pay off their debts. But the price of oil in early 1990 was very low. In August 1990, Saddam Hussein suddenly invaded and conquered his oil-rich neighbor, tiny *Kuwait*.

SAW-dee ah-RAY-be-ah

Kuh-WAIT

The world gasped at Saddam's bold, **reckless** move. Countries worried about losing their supply of oil from the Middle East. Without oil, industries, transportation, everything would come to a halt. The United States also buys a lot of oil from the Middle East because it is cheap and plentiful. We, too, were worried.

President George Bush warned Saddam Hussein over and over to "get out of Kuwait!" The United Nations, which is the world's peace-keeping organization, also demanded that Iraq withdraw. The United States quickly sent troops to protect Saudi Arabia, a neighbor that Iraq might threaten.

In the months that followed, other countries also sent troops and equipment to the Middle East. As in the Korean War, America supplied most of the United Nations armed forces. General Colin Powell, chairman of the Joint Chiefs of Staff, called on General Norman *Schwarzkopf* to be the chief American military commander. Over half a million United States service men and women were sent to the hot Saudi Arabian desert.

SCHWARTZ-cough

At first, the United States and its allies tried to avoid open war with Iraq. They organized an air and naval blockade of the country. This made it hard for the Iraqis to buy food or medical supplies, or to sell their oil. It was hoped that these **sanctions** would force Iraq to get out of Kuwait without a shot being fired.

Two months later, President Bush and some of his advisers became impatient with the sanctions. Other leaders warned that it would take at least six months for the sanctions to work. But Bush urged the UN to act before more scorching hot weather returned to the desert. In November 1990 the UN set a deadline of January 15, 1991, for Iraq to leave Kuwait. If Saddam Hussein failed to do so, the UN would "use all necessary means," including force, to drive him out.

Iraq's leader paid no attention to the threat. Perhaps he did not believe that the United States would fight his country. After all, we had supported Iraq during the 1980s in its war against Iran. We had provided aid, which helped Saddam Hussein to build up a powerful war machine.

Meanwhile, President Bush held telephone talks with President Gorbachev. The Soviet leader was friendly and helpful. He had no plans to support Iraq against the United States and to start up the Cold War again. He agreed that Iraq should get out of Kuwait.

When the January deadline passed, the United States and its UN allies attacked Iraq. The military operation was called Desert Storm. American planes bombed Iraq day and night for a month. Great damage was done to the country and its people. Roads, bridges, oil refineries, and electric power plants were destroyed. Then tanks and foot soldiers crushed the Iraqi army, taking thousands of prisoners. Saddam Hussein pulled his forces out of Kuwait as President Bush and the United Nations had ordered.

Late in February 1991, the Persian Gulf War stopped, but violence continued. Saddam Hussein remained in power, crushing bloody revolts of his people. Also, Iraq still had dangerous nuclear and chemical weapons hidden. The UN sent teams of scientists to hunt for these killer weapons. Angry Iraqis tried to block the scientists from carrying out their orders. ●

In the early 1990s, many of the republics in the Soviet Union wanted freedom and democracy in their lands. Communist government officials made a last-ditch effort to save the Soviet Union. They surprised and captured President Gorbachev, whom they no longer trusted. They planned to run the government themselves. But within a few days Gorbachev was rescued by his old rival, Boris Yeltsin.

Yeltsin had become president of Russia in a democratic election. He did not want to see communism returned to Russia, the largest of the republics. Boldly, Yeltsin climbed on top of an army tank in Moscow to speak to the people gathered in the street. He told his listeners to disobey the new leaders. He said that Gorbachev must be freed and returned to Moscow. Throughout the republics, both soldiers and civilians opposed the new leaders. In a few days Gorbachev returned to Moscow. From that moment of triumph, Boris Yeltsin was a hero and the most important figure in the new republics.

Once freed, Gorbachev still hoped to rebuild the Communist Party and to keep the republics together. But the people said no. One after another, many of the republics declared independence. By December 1991 there was no Soviet Union of which Gorbachev could be president. Sadly, he resigned.

Although this was seen as a victory for democracy, Yeltsin and the other leaders in the independent republics faced serious problems. Times were very hard. Then, too, the people living in these new nations were a mixture of different races, religions, and languages. Often they could not get along with each other. Bloody fighting broke out in the former republics and in parts of eastern Europe which also had been under Soviet rule.

In all this confusion, the former Soviets looked to the United States for help. Russia needed food and money, which we began sending. Many Americans agreed that helping Russia was important to keep democracy alive. Otherwise a dictator might overthrow Yeltsin and start a new Cold War with America. ●

The United States was also having hard times in the 1990s. Foreign trade was very important to us. Factories made goods to sell abroad, which meant jobs and comfortable times for our people. But during the 1980s foreign trade moved the other way. Japan and other countries sold us far more goods than we sold them. As a result, the United States owed large amounts of money abroad. Other countries loaned us money to pay our debts and bought up some important American businesses and real estate. Meanwhile, many defense plants and factories shut down because there was less demand for their products.

The unemployment problem was hard to solve. Some people suggested a public works program to give jobs to the unemployed. The country was badly in need of new highways, bridges, airports, schools, and housing. There was also talk about retraining defense workers to make peacetime products instead of guns and other weapons. The growing field of waste management and environmental clean-up was an example. If skilled workers could be retrained to manufacture equipment to help clean up pollution, the country might again be able to find good markets for selling their products. But both public works and retraining programs cost money, and the United States was deeply in debt.

Throughout the 1980s the government was running on an unbalanced **budget**. This means it spent more money than it took in. There are two ways the government can balance the budget and get out of debt. First, it can spend less money on federal programs, such as Medicare, education, and defense. Second, it can raise taxes to bring in money to pay for these and other services.

Neither way is popular with the American people. They want the government to help them when they need it. At the same time they complain about higher taxes to pay for these programs.

Under Presidents Reagan and Bush there was more expense-cutting (except in defense-spending, which increased) than tax-raising to meet people's needs. As a result, programs that the people had counted on were cut back. Just as important, programs that had not started yet, like health care, had to be delayed. ●

For all the troubles America faced in the early 1990s, there was hope for the future. The threat of a big war was gone. Democracy was

in the march. There was the promise of a "new world order," perhaps
led by the United Nations. Whatever happened, Americans remained
hopeful that under their new president, Bill Clinton, they could meet
the challenges that lay ahead.

Answer these to review the main ideas.

1. How did President Reagan feel about the Soviet Union and

   communism? _____

   _____

   _____

2. Who is Mikhail Gorbachev? How was he different from other Soviet

   leaders? _____

   _____

   _____

3. Who won the Cold War? _____

   _____

   _____

4. Why did President Bush order Saddam Hussein to get out of Kuwait?

   What happened to Saddam and Iraq? _____

   _____

   _____

5. Who is Boris Yeltsin? _____

   _____

   _____

6. What problems did the United States face in the 1990s? _____

   _____

   _____

A.

Circle the right answer to finish each sentence.

B.

1. The "evil empire" was President Reagan's name for

   a. Japan   b. the Soviet   c. China
                             Union

2. Mikhail Gorbachev wanted to

   a. end the Cold War   b. increase military   c. fight to
       with the U.S.   spending   the end

3. The Middle East is rich in

   a. iron   b. lumber   c. oil

4. The chairman of the Joint Chiefs of Staff in 1990 was

   a. Dwight   b. Colin Powell   c. Ronald Reagan
       Eisenhower

5. Boris Yeltsin was elected the first president of

   a. the Soviet   b. the Russian   c. the United
       Union   Republic   Nations

Circle True or False.

C.

T F   1. President Reagan was against building up America's military strength.

T F   2. Mikhail Gorbachev wanted both the United States and the Soviet Union to cut military spending.

T F   3. The United States and the United Nations attacked Iraq in the Persian Gulf War.

T F   4. At the end of the Cold War, Russia was rich and prosperous.

T F   5. In the 1990s, America's foreign trade declined, and the United States went deeply into debt.

Choose one of these words to fit each sentence below.

D.

strut   sanctions   scowling

bankrupt   reckless   budget

1. Many countries thought Iraq was _____ to invade Kuwait.

2. If you spend or lose your money and can't pay what you owe, you are

_____.

Before the Persian Gulf War, the United Nations used

_____ against Iraq.

"Stop _____ at me," the girl told her angry friend.

We watched the band members _____ down the street in the July Fourth parade.

To have a balanced _____, the government must not spend more money than it takes in.

E.

Think about and discuss in class.

The United States and its United Nations allies drove Iraq out of Kuwait, then stopped fighting. Should we have continued the war until Iraq was conquered and Saddam Hussein overthrown? What is happening in Iraq today? _____

_____

_____

Some people think that the United States spends too much money helping other countries and not enough on our own people. They say that Americans need better schools, health care, jobs, and other social programs. Do you agree with this view, or should we continue foreign spending in order to remain a world leader? _____

_____

_____

In recent years Japan sold the United States far more goods than we sold them. Why wasn't America able to compete more successfully with Japan in foreign trade? _____

_____

_____

_____

What do you suppose happens to countries that spend more money than they take in?

_____

_____